By Ajit Singh & Bhawna Sinha

Core Java
Simply In Depth

ISBN: 9781981098248

AKNOWLEDGEMENT

This piece of study of **Core Java** is an outcome of the encouragement, guidance, help and assistance provided to us by our colleagues, faculties, Tech-friends and our family members.

As an aknowledgement, we would like to take the opportunity to express our deep sense of gratitude to all those who played a crucial role in the successful completion of this book, especially to our sr. students; this book certainly has been benefited from discussions held with many IT professionals (Ex-students) over the years it took us to write it.

Our primary goal is to provide a sufficient introduction and details of the Core Java, incuding the features of Java 8 so that the students can have an efficient knowledge about Core Java. Moreover, it presupposes knowledge of the principles and concepts of the C++ language is required. On the same note, any errors and inaccuracies are our responsibility and any suggestions in this regard are warmly welcomed!

We would like to thank our mentor and valued guardian, *Prof Dr. Bal Gangadhar Prasad* (HOD-Dept of Mathematics, Patna University) for setting a very high standard of writing about programming and for providing valuable suggestions in practical language design of this book.

Finally, We would like to thank the **Kindle Direct Publishing** team and **Amazon** team for its enthusiastic online support and guidance in bringing out this book.

We hope that the reader likes this book and finds it useful in learning the concepts of Core Java.

Thank You !!

Ajit Singh & Bhawna Sinha

PREFACE

The study/learning of Core Java is an essential part of any computer science education and of course for the B.Tech / MCA / M.Tech courses of several Universities across the world. This textbook is intended as a text for an explanatory course of Core Java for Graduate and Post Graduate students of several universities across the world.

To The Student

This text is an introduction to the complex world of the Java Technologies. This book encapsulates rich practical hands-on experience in developing web applications, combined with teaching the subject for graduate/post-graduate students. The book is therefore a culmination of putting together what has been both practiced as well as preached, which is the one of the most compelling differentiators for this book. But what is more fascinating is the nature of the web itself. It can also be used for independent study by anyone interested in getting a broad introduction to a core useful subset of the many technologies of Java.

Our approach in this book is to regard Java as a language that readers will want to use as a primary tool in many different areas of their programming work - not just for creating programs with graphical content within Web pages. For this reason, in the early chapters we have avoided an emphasis on creating applets and GUI-based programs. While being able to create GUI-based programs is superficially attractive, the language concepts required to create them properly are, in fact, quite advanced. Nevertheless, we recognize that visual examples are much more fun to create and work with.

Key Features

The following are key features of this book:

- An 'objects-early' approach; showing how to interact with fully-fledged objects, before moving on, in Chapter 4, to define classes from scratch.
- An accessible introduction to the fundamental object-oriented topics of *polymorphism* and *inheritance*.

- Significant coverage of the many GUI classes belonging to both the Abstract Windowing Toolkit (AWT) and Swing (JFC), which support both *standalone applications* and *applets*.
- Up-to-date coverage of the Java 2 Platform API including the features of Java 8.
- How to use the power of *threads* for multi-threaded programs, while avoiding hazards such as deadlock, livelock and thread starvation.
- A unique chapter on event-driven simulation.

Feedback

We have attempted to wash out every error in our first edition of this book after being reviewed by lots of scholars of Computer Science, but as happens with Programmig – "A few bugs difficult to understand shall remain" – and therefore, suggestions from students that may lead to improvement of next edition in shortcoming future are highly appreciated.

*Conclusive suggestions and criticism always go a long way in enhancing any endeavour. We request all readers to email us their valuable comments / views / feedback for the betterment of the book at **bhawna.sahay2004@gmail.com / ajit_singh24@yahoo.com** mentioning the title and author name in the subject line. Please report any piracy spotted by you as well . We would be glad to hear suggestions from you.*

We hope, you enjoy reading this book as much as we have enjoyed writing it. We would be glad to hear suggestions from you.

About the Author(s)

Ajit Singh

Ajit is currently a Ph.D candidate at Magadh University, Bihar, IND working on Social Media Predictive Data Analytics at the A. N. College Research Centre, Patna, IND, under the supervision of **_Prof Dr Manish Kumar_** (Associate Professor-Dept of Mathematics, A. N. College, MU, Bihar).

He also holds M.Phil. degree in Computer Science, and is a Microsoft MCSE / MCDBA / MCSD.. He has 18 years of strong teaching experience of graduate and under graduate courses of Computer Science in Patna University. His main area of interests are in programming languages, Network Security, Automata Theory and Operating Systems.

Ajit can be contacted via one of two places:
http://facebook.com/ajitseries
http://amazon.com/author/ajitsingh

Email: ajit_singh24@yahoo.com
Ph: +91-92-346-11498

Dr. Bhawna Sinha

Dr. Bhawna Sinha (MCA, M.Phil, Ph.D) is currently working as Asst. Professor at Patna Women's College, Patna University. She has around 21 years of teaching experience and is currently heading the MCA Department.

Her area of interest is Fuzzy Computing, Data mining, Computer Organization and Computer Networks.

She is a life member of CSI and was also awarded *Active Woman Member of CSI* in the year 2016. She has published several papers in both international and national levels and edited three books *"Computer Literacy: An Overview"*, *"3D Animation and Design"* and *"Web Designing"*. She is involved in various academic and administrative activities and is a member of Research Committee and IQAC of the College.

Bhawna can be contacted via:

E-mail: bhawna.sahay2004@gmail.com

CONTENTS

1

INTRODUCTION TO JAVA

Unit Structure
Introduction
Basic concepts of OOPs
Java History
Java Feature
Comparison in Java and C++
Java Virtual Machine
Java Environment
Program
Summary

1.1 INTRODUCTION:

Java is a high-level, third generation programming language, like C, FORTRAN, Smalltalk, Perl, and many others. You can use Java to write computer applications that play games, store data or do any of the thousands of other things computer software can do. Compared to other programming languages, Java is most similar to C. However although Java shares much of C's syntax, it is not C. Knowing how to program in C or, better yet, C++, will certainly help you to learn Java more quickly, but you don't need to know C to learn Java. A Java compiler won't compile C code, and most large C programs need to be changed substantially before they can become Java programs. What's most special about Java in relation to other programming languages is that it lets you write special programs called applets that can be downloaded from the Internet and played safely within a web browser. Java language is called as an Object-Oriented Programming language and before begining for Java, we have to learn the concept of OOPs(Object-Oriented Programming).

1.2 BASIC CONCEPT OF OOPS (OBJECT-ORIENTED PROGRAMMING):

There are some basic concepts of object oriented programming as follows:
- Object
- Class
- Data abstraction
- Data encapsulation
- Inheritance
- Polymorphism
- Dynamic binding

1. Object
Objects are important runtime entities in object oriented method. They may characterize a location, a bank account, and a table of data or any entry that the program must handle.
For example:

Object: STUDENT
DATA
Name
Address
Marks
METHODS
Total ()
Average ()

Fig.1.1 Representation of an object "STUDENT"

Each object holds data and code to operate the data. Object can interact without having to identify the details of each other's data or code. It is sufficient to identify the type of message received and the type of reply returned by the objects.
Another example of object is CAR

Object: CAR
DATA
Colour
Cost
METHODS
LockIt ()
DriveIt ()

Fig.1.2 Representation of object "CAR"
Fig.1.1 and Fig.1.2 shows actual representation of object.

2. Classes

A class is a set of objects with similar properties (attributes), common behaviour (operations), and common link to other objects.The complete set of data and code of an object can be made a user defined data type with the help of class.

The objects are variable of type class. A class is a collection of objects of similar type. Classes are user defined data types and work like the build in type of the programming language. Once the class has been defined, we can make any number of objects belonging to that class. Each object is related with the data of type class with which they are formed.

As we learned that, the classification of objects into various classes is based on its properties (States) and behaviour (methods). Classes are used to distinguish are type of object from another. The important thing about the class is to identify the properties and procedures and applicability to its instances.

For example: Vehicle

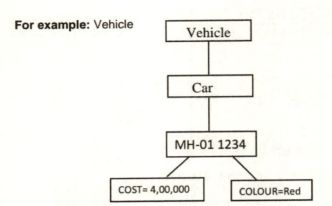

Fig.1.3 Representation of class

In above example, we will create an objects MH-01 1234 belonging to the class car. The objects develop their distinctiveness from the difference in their attribute value and relationships to other objects.

3. Data Abstraction
Data abstraction refers to the act of representing important description without including the background details or explanations.

Classes use the concept of abstraction and are defined as a list of abstract attributes such as size, cost and functions operate on these attributes. They summarize all the important properties of the objects that are to be created.

Classes use the concepts of data abstraction and it is called as Abstract Data Type (ADT).

4. Data Encapsulation
Data Encapsulation means wrapping of data and functions into a single unit (i.e. class). It is most useful feature of class. The data is not easy to get to the outside world and only those functions which are enclosed in the class can access it.

These functions provide the boundary between Object's data and program. This insulation of data from direct access by the program is called as **Data hiding**.

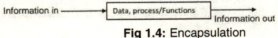

Fig 1.4: Encapsulation

5. Inheritance
Inheritance is the process by which objects of one class can get the properties of objects of another class. Inheritance means one class of objects inherits the data and behaviours from another class. Inheritance maintains the hierarchical classification in which a class inherits from its parents.

Inheritance provides the important feature of OOP that is reusability. That means we can include additional characteristics to an existing class without modification. This is possible deriving a new class from existing one.

In other words, it is property of object-oriented systems that allow objects to be built from other objects. Inheritance allows openly taking help of the commonality of objects when constructing new classes. Inheritance is a relationship between classes where one class is the parent class of another (derived) class. The derived class holds the properties and behaviour of base class in addition to the properties and behaviour of derived class.

For Example:

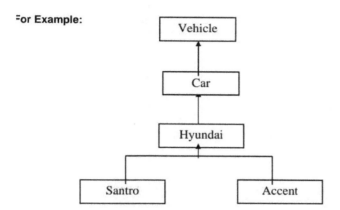

Fig.1.5 Inheritance

In Fig.1.5, the Santro is a part of the class Hyundai which is again part of the class car and car is the part of the class vehicle. That means vehicle class is the parent class.

6. Polymorphism
(Poly means "many" and morph means "form"). Polymorphism means the ability to take more than one form. Polymorphism plays a main role in allocate objects having different internal structures to share the same external interface. This means that a general class of operations may be accessed in the same manner even though specific activities associated with each operation may differ. Polymorphism is broadly used in implementing inheritance.

It means objects that can take on or assume many different forms. Polymorphism means that the same operations may behave differently on different classes. Booch defines polymorphism as the relationship of objects many different classes by some common super class. Polymorphism allows us to write generic, reusable code more easily, because we can specify general instructions and delegate the implementation detail to the objects involved.

For Example:

In a pay roll system, manager, office staff and production worker objects all will respond to the compute payroll message, but the real operations performed are object particular.

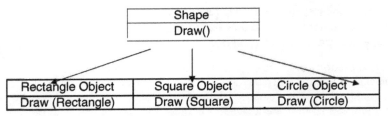

Shape		
Draw()		
Rectangle Object	Square Object	Circle Object
Draw (Rectangle)	Draw (Square)	Draw (Circle)

Fig.1.6 Polymorphism

7. Dynamic Binding

Binding refers to the linking of a procedure call to the code to be executed in response to the call. Dynamic binding means that the code related with a given procedure call is not known until the time of the call at run time.

Dynamic binding is associated polymorphism and inheritance.

1.3 JAVA HISTORY :

Java is a general-purpose, object-oriented programming language developed by Sun Microsystems of USA in 1991.Originally called Oak by James Gosling (one of the inventor of the language). Java was invented for the development of software for cunsumer electronic devices like TVs, tosters, etc. The main aim had to make java simple, portable and reliable. Java Authors: James , Arthur Van , and others.

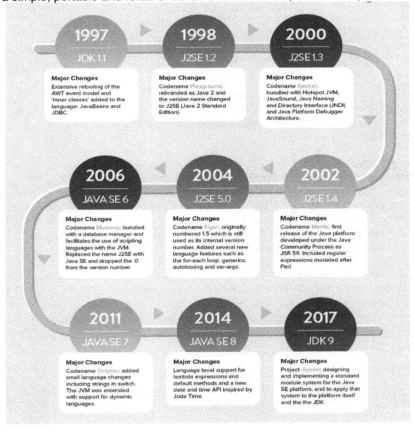

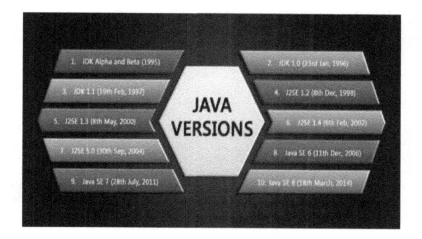

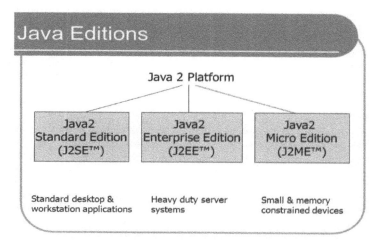

1.4 JAVA FEATURES:

As we know that the Java is an object oriented programming language developed by Sun Microsystems of USA in 1991. Java is first programming language which is not attached with any particular hardware or operating system. Program developed in Java can be executed anywhere and on any system. Features of Java are as follows:

- Compiled and Interpreted
- Platform Independent and portable
- Object- oriented
- Robust and secure
- Distributed
- Familiar, simple and small
- Multithreaded and Interactive
- High performance
- Dynamic and Extensible

1. Compiled and Interpreted

Basically a computer language is either compiled or interpreted. Java comes together both these approach thus making Java a two-stage system.

Java compiler translates Java code to Bytecode instructions and Java Interpreter generate machine code that can be directly executed by machine that is running the Java program.

2. Platform Independent and portable

Java supports the feature portability. Java programs can be easily moved from one computer system to another and anywhere. Changes and upgrades in operating systems, processors and system resources will not force any alteration in Java programs. This is reason why Java has become a trendy language for programming on Internet which interconnects different kind of systems worldwide. Java certifies portability in two ways.

First way is, Java compiler generates the bytecode and that can be executed on any machine. Second way is, size of primitive data types are machine independent.

3. Object- oriented

Java is truly object-oriented language. In Java, almost everything is an Object. All program code and data exist in objects and classes. Java comes with an extensive set of classes; organize in packages that can be used in program by Inheritance. The object model in Java is trouble-free and easy to enlarge.

4. Robust and secure

Java is a most strong language which provides many securities to make certain reliable code. It is design as garbage – collected language, which helps the programmers virtually from all memory management problems. Java also includes the concept of exception handling, which detain serious errors and reduces all kind of threat of crashing the system.

Security is an important feature of Java and this is the strong reason that programmer use this language for programming on Internet.

The absence of pointers in Java ensures that programs cannot get right of entry to memory location without proper approval.

5. Distributed

Java is called as Distributed language for construct applications on networks which can contribute both data and programs. Java applications can open and access remote objects on Internet easily. That means multiple programmers at multiple remote locations to work together on single task.

6. Simple and small

Java is very small and simple language. Java does not use pointer and header files, goto statements, etc. It eliminates operator overloading and multiple inheritance.

7. Multithreaded and Interactive

Multithreaded means managing multiple tasks simultaneously. Java maintains multithreaded programs. That means we need not wait for the application to complete one task before starting next task. This feature is helpful for graphic applications.

8. High performance

Java performance is very extraordinary for an interpreted language, majorly due to the use of intermediate bytecode. Java architecture is also designed to reduce overheads during runtime. The incorporation of multithreading improves the execution speed of program.

9. Dynamic and Extensible

Java is also dynamic language. Java is capable of dynamically linking in new class, libraries, methods and objects. Java can also establish the type of class through the query building it possible to either dynamically link or abort the program, depending on the reply.

Java program is support functions written in other language such as C and C++, known as native methods.

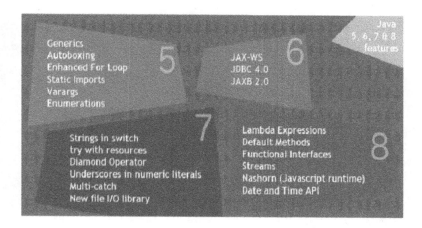

1.5 JAVA ENVIRONMENT:

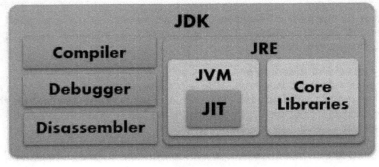

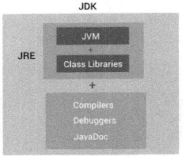

Java environment includes a number of development tools, classes and methods. The development tools are part of the system known as Java Development Kit (JDK) and the classes and methods are part of the Java Standard Library (JSL), also known as the Application Programming Interface (API).

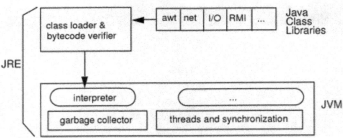

Java Development kit (JDK) – The JDK comes with a set of tools that are used for developing and running Java program. It includes:

- o Appletviewer(It is used for viewing the applet)
- o Javac(It is a Java Compiler)
- o Java(It is a java interpreter)
- o Javap(Java diassembler,which convert byte code into program description)
- o Javah(It is for java C header files)
- o Javadoc(It is for creating HTML document)
- o Jdb(It is Java debugger)

1.6 JAVA VIRTUAL MACHINE:

As we know that all programming language compilers convert the source code to machine code.Same job done by Java Compiler to run a Java program, but the difference is that Java compiler convert the source code into Intermediate code is called as bytecode. This machine is called the *Java Virtual machine* and it exits only inside the computer memory.

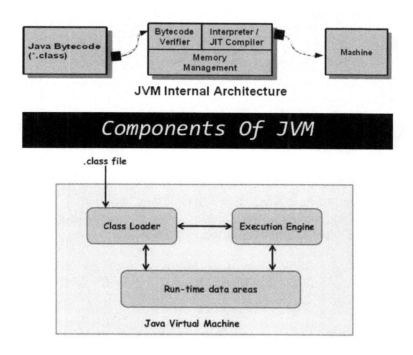

Following figure shows the process of compilation.

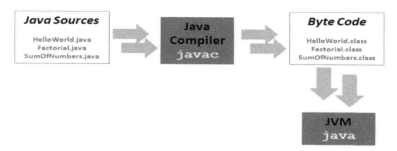

The Virtual machine code is not machine specific. The machine specific code is generated. By Java interpreter by acting as an intermediary between the virtual machine and real machines shown below

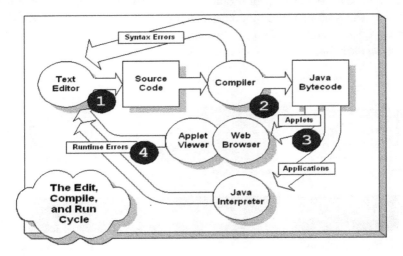

Java Object Framework act as the intermediary between the user programs and the virtual machine which in turn act as the intermediary between the operating system and the Java Object Framework.

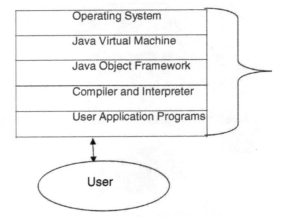

Fig: Layers of Interaction for Java programs

Difference between JDK, JRE and JVM

1. Brief summary of JVM
2. Java Runtime Environment (JRE)
3. Java Development Kit (JDK)

We must understand the differences between JDK, JRE and JVM before proceeding further to Java.

JVM

JVM (Java Virtual Machine) is an abstract machine. It is a specification that provides runtime environment in which java bytecode can be executed.

JVMs are available for many hardware and software platforms. JVM, JRE and JDK are platform dependent because configuration of each OS differs. But, Java is platform independent. There are three notions of the JVM: specification, implementation, and instance.

The JVM performs following main tasks:

○ Loads code
○ Verifies code
○ Executes code
○ Provides runtime environment

JRE

JRE is an acronym for Java Runtime Environment. It is used to provide runtime environment. It is the implementation of JVM. It physically exists. It contains set of libraries + other files that JVM uses at runtime.

Implementation of JVMs are also actively released by other companies besides Sun Micro Systems.

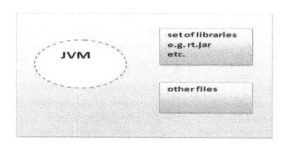

JRE

JDK

JDK is an acronym for Java Development Kit. It physically exists. It contains JRE + development tools.

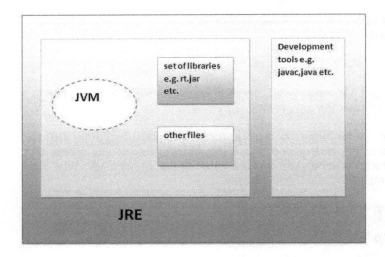

JDK

1.7 Download, Install & Configure Java JDK in Windows

This Java Development Kit(JDK) allows you to code and run Java programs. It's possible that you install multiple JDK versions on the same PC. But Its recommended that you install only latest version.

Following are steps to install Java in Windows

Step 1: Download JDK

1. Goto Java SE download site
   http://www.oracle.com/technetwork/java/javase/downloads/index.html

2. Under "Java Platform, Standard Edition" ⇒ "Java SE 10.0.{x}", where {x} denotes a fast   running update number ⇒ Click the JDK's "Download" button.

3. Under "Java SE Development Kit 10.0.{x}" ⇒ Check "Accept License Agreement".

4. Choose the JDK for your operating system, i.e., "Windows" (for 64-bit Windows OS), and download the installer (e.g., "jdk-10.0.{x}_windows-x64_bin.exe" - 390MB).

Step 2: Install JDK and JRE

Run the downloaded installer (e.g., "jdk-10.0.{x}_windows-x64_bin.exe"), which installs both the JDK and JRE.

By default:

- JDK is installed in directory "C:\Program Files\Java\jdk-10.0.{x}", where {x} denotes the upgrade number; and
- JRE is installed in "C:\Program Files\Java\jre-10.0.{x}".

Notes: In 64-bit Windows, "Program Files" is meant for 64-bit programs; while "Program Files (x86)" for 32-bit programs.

Accept the defaults and follow the screen instructions to install JDK and JRE.

Use the "File Explorer", goto "C:\Program Files\Java" to inspect these folders. Take note of your **JDK installed directory**, in particular, the varying upgrade number, which you will need in the next step.

In the following diagram, the JDK installed directory is "C:\Program Files\Java\jdk-10.0.1", where {x}=1. I shall refer to the **JDK installed directory** as **<JAVA_HOME>**, hereafter, in this article.

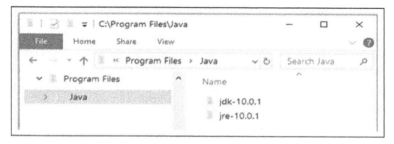

Step 3: Include JDK's "bin" Directory in the PATH

Windows' Shell searches the current directory and the directories listed in the PATH *environment variable* (*system variable*) for executable programs. JDK's programs (such as Java compiler javac.exe and Java runtime java.exe) reside in the *sub-directory* "bin" of the JDK installed directory. You need to include "bin" in the PATH to run the JDK programs.

To edit the PATH environment variable in Windows 7/8/10:

1. Launch "Control Panel" ⇒ (Optional) System and Security ⇒ System ⇒ Click "Advanced system settings" on the left pane.
2. Switch to "Advanced" tab ⇒ Push "Environment Variables" button.
3. Under "System Variables" (the bottom pane), scroll down to select "Path" ⇒ Click "Edit...".
4. **For Windows 10 (newer releases)**:
   You shall see a **TABLE** listing all the existing PATH entries (if not, goto next step). Click "New" ⇒ Enter the JDK's "bin" directory "c:\Program Files\Java\jdk-10.0.{x}**bin**" (Replace {x} with your installation number!!!) ⇒ Select "Move Up" to move this entry all the way to the TOP.

   Prior to newer Windows 10:

(CAUTION: Read this paragraph 3 times before doing this step! Don't push "Apply" or "OK" until you are 101% sure. There is no UNDO!!!)
(To be SAFE, copy the content of the "Variable value" to Notepad before changing it!!!)
In "Variable value" field, <u>INSERT</u> "c:\Program Files\Java\jdk-10.0.{x}\bin" (Replace {x} with your installation number!!!) <u>IN FRONT</u> of all the existing directories, <u>followed by a semi-colon (;)</u> which separates the JDK's bin directory from the rest of the existing directories. <u>DO NOT DELETE</u> any existing entries; otherwise, some existing applications may not run.

Variable name : PATH

Variable value : c:\Program Files\Java\jdk-10.0.{x}\bin;[*do not delete exiting entries...*]

Notes: Starting from JDK 1.8, the installation created a directory "c:\ProgramData\Oracle\Java\javapath" and added to the PATH. It contains only JRE executables (java.exe, javaw.exe, and javaws.exe), but NOT the JDK executables (e.g., javac.exe).

Step 4: Verify the JDK Installation

Launch a CMD shell via one of the following means:

1. Click "Search" button ⇒ Enter "cmd" ⇒ Choose "Command Prompt", or
2. right-click "Start" button ⇒ run... ⇒enter "cmd", or
3. (Prior to Windows 10) click "Start" button ⇒ All Programs ⇒ Accessories (or Windows System) ⇒Command Prompt, or
4. (Windows 10) click "Start" button ⇒Windows System ⇒Command Prompt.

Issue the following commands to verify your JDK installation:

1. Issue "path" command to list the contents of the PATH environment variable. Check to make sure that your <JAVA_HOME>\bin is listed in the PATH. Don't type prompt>, which denotes the command prompt!!! Key in the command (highlighted) only.

2. // Display the PATH entries

3. prompt> **path**

PATH=c:\Program Files\Java\jdk-10.0.{x}\bin;[*other entries...*]

4. Issue the following commands to verify that JDK/JRE are properly installed and display their version:

5. // Display the JRE version

6. prompt> **java -version**

7. java version "10.0.{x}" 2018-04-17

8. Java(TM) SE Runtime Environment 18.3 (build 10.0.1+10)

9. Java HotSpot(TM) 64-Bit Server VM 18.3 (build 10.0.1+10, mixed mode)

10. // Display the JDK version

11.   prompt> **javac -version**

javac 10.0.{x}

[Optional]How To Set the Environment Variable JAVA_HOME

Many Java applications (such as Tomcat) require the environment variable JAVA_HOME to be set to the JDK installed directory.

To set the JAVA_HOME environment variable:

1. First, find your JDK installed directory. For JDK 10, the default is "c:\Program Files\Java\jdk-10.0.xx", where xx is the upgrade number. Use your "File Explorer" to view this directory and take note of your JDK installed directory.

2. Check if JAVA_HOME is already set. Start a CMD and issue:

   SET JAVA_HOME
   If you get a message "Environment variable JAVA_HOME not defined", proceed to the   next   step.
   If you get "JAVA_HOME=C:\Program Files\Java\jdk-10.0.{x}", verify that it is set correctly to your JDK directory. If not, proceed to the next step.

3. To set the environment variable JAVA_HOME in Windows 10/8/7: Launch "Control Panel" ⇒ (Optional) System and Security ⇒ System ⇒ Advanced system settings ⇒ Switch to "Advanced" tab ⇒ Environment Variables ⇒ System Variables (the bottom pane) ⇒ "New" (or look for "JAVA_HOME" and "Edit" if it is already set) ⇒ In "Variable Name", enter "JAVA_HOME" ⇒ In "Variable Value", enter your JDK installed directory you noted in Step 1. (In the latest Windows 10: you can push the "Browse Directory..." button and select the JDK installed directory to avoid typo error.)

4. To verify, **RE-START** a CMD (restart needed to refresh the environment) and issue:

5.   **SET JAVA_HOME**

JAVA_HOME=c:\Program Files\Java\jdk-10.0.{x}   <== Verify that this is YOUR JDK installed directory

Notes: Windows' environment variables (such as JAVA_HOME, PATH) are NOT case-sensitive.

1.8 SIMPLE JAVA PROGRAM:

For compiling and running the program we have to use following commands:
   a) **javac (Java compiler)**

In java, we can use any text editor for writing program and then save that program with ".java" extension. Java compiler convert the source code or program in bytecode and interpreter convert ".java" file in ".class" file.
Syntax:
C:\javac filename.java
If my filename is "abc.java" then the syntax will be
C:\javac abc.java

   b) **java(Java Interpreter)**

As we learn that, we can use any text editor for writing program and then save that program with ".java" extension. Java compiler convert the source code or program in bytecode and interpreter convert ".java" file in ".class" file.
Syntax:
C:\java filename
If my filename is abc.java then the syntax will be C:\java abc

```
class FirstProgram
    {
        public static void main(String args[])
        {
        System.out.println ("This is my first program");
        }
    }
```

- The file must be named "FirstProgram.java" to equivalent the class name containing the main method.
- Java is case sensitive. This program defines a class called "FirstProgram".
- A class is an object oriented term. It is designed to perform a specific task. A Java class is defined by its class name, an open curly brace, a list of methods and fields, and a close curly brace.
- The name of the class is made of alphabetical characters and digits without spaces, the first character must be alphabetical.
- The line "public static void main (String [] args)" shows where the program will start running. The word main means that this is the main method –
- The JVM starts running any program by executing this method first.
- The main method in "FirstProgram.java" consists of a single statement System.out. println ("This is my first program");
- The statement outputs the character between quotes to the console.

Above explanation is about how to write program and now we have to learn where to write program and how to compile and run the program.

For this reason, the next explanation is showing the steps.
1. Edit the program by the use of Notepad.
2. Save the program to the hard disk.
3. Compile the program with the javac command.(Java compiler)
4. If there are syntax errors, go back to Notepad and edit the program.
5. Run the program with the java command.(Java Interpreter)
6. If it does not run correctly, go back to Notepad and edit the program.
7. When it shows result then stop.

What is Java bytecode?

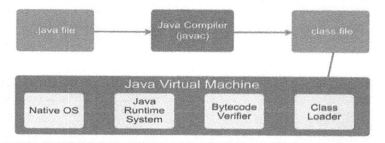

Java VM Platforms

Bytecode Ensures Architecture Neutrality

Chip Architectures
- Intel x86
- Intel/AMD x64
- IBM Power
- HP PA-RISC
- ARM
- Sparc
- Itanium

Plus more...

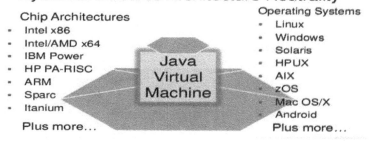

Operating Systems
- Linux
- Windows
- Solaris
- HPUX
- AIX
- zOS
- Mac OS/X
- Android

Plus more...

1.9 COMPARISON IN C, C++ And JAVA

Aspects	C	C++	Java
Developed Year	1972	1979	1991
Developed By	Dennis Ritchie	Bjarne Stroustrup	James Gosling
Successor of	BCPL	C	C(Syntax) & C++ (Structure)
Paradigms	Procedural	Object Oriented	Object Oriented
Platform Dependency	Dependent	Dependent	Independent
Keywords	32	63	50 defined (goto, const unusable)
Datatypes : union, structure	Supported	Supported	Not Supported
Pre-processor directives	Supported (#include, #define)	Supported (#include, #define)	Not Supported
Header files	Supported	Supported	Use Packages (import)
Inheritance	No Inheritance	Supported	Multiple Inheritance not Supported
Overloading	No Overloading	Supported	Operator Overloading not Supported
Pointers	Supported	Supported	No Pointers
Code Translation	Compiled	Compiled	Interpreted
Storage Allocation	Uses malloc, calloc	Uses new , delete	uses garbage collector
Multi-threading and Interfaces	Not Supported	Not Supported	Supported
Exception Handling	No Exception handling	Supported	Supported
Templates	Not Supported	Supported	Not Supported
Storage class: auto, extern	Supported	Supported	Not Supported
Destructors	No Constructor or Destructor	Supported	Not Supported
Database Connectivity	Not Supported	Not Supported	Supported

SUMMARY :

In this unit, we learn the concept of Object Oriented Programming, Introduction of Java, History of Java, Features of Java, Comparison between C++ and Java, Java virtual Machine and Java Environment.

2

DATA TYPES, VARIABLES AND CONSTANTS

DATA TYPES:

A **data type** is a scheme for representing values. An example is int which is the Integer, a data type.
Values are not just numbers, but any manner of data that a computer can process.
The data type defines the kind of data that is represented by a variable.
As with the keyword class, Java data types are case sensitive.
    There are two types of data types
        o   primitive data type
        o   non-pimitive data type

In primitive data types, there are two categories
        o   numeric means Integer, Floating points
        o   Non-numeric means Character and Boolean

In non-pimitive types, there are three categories
        o   classes
        o   arrays
        o   interface

Following table shows the datatypes with their size and ranges.

Data type	Size (byte)	Range
byte	1	-128 to 127
boolean	1	True or false
char	2	A-Z,a-z,0-9,etc.
short	2	-32768 to 32767
Int	4	(about) -2 million to 2 million
long	8	(about) -10E18 to 10E18
float	4	-3.4E38 to 3.4E18
double	8	-1.7E308 to 1.7E308

Fig: Datatypes with size and range

Integer data type:

Integer datatype can hold the numbers (the number can be positive number or negative number). In Java, there are four types of integer as follows:

- byte
- short
- int
- long

We can make ineger long by adding 'l' or 'L' at the end of the number.

2.1.2 Floating point data type:

It is also called as Real number and when we require accuracy then we can use it. There are two types of floating point data type.

- float
- double

It is represent single and double precision numbers. The float type is used for single precision and it uses 4 bytes for storage space. It is very useful when we require accuracy with small degree of precision. But in double type, it is used for double precision and uses 8 bytes of starage space. It is useful for large degree of precision.

2.1.3 Character data type:

It is used to store single character in memory. It uses 2 bytes storage space.

2.1.4 Boolean data type:

It is used when we want to test a particular condition during the excution of the program. There are only two values that a boolean type can hold: true and false. Boolean type is denoted by the keyword boolean and uses only one bit of storage.

Following program shows the use of datatypes.

Program:

```
import java.io.DataInputStream;
class cc2
{
public static void main(String args[]) throws Exception
{
DataInputStream s1=new DataInputStream(System.in);
byte rollno;
int marks1,marks2,marks3; float avg;
```

```
System.out.println("Enter roll number:");
rollno=Byte.parseByte(s1.readLine());
System.out.println("Enter marks m1, m2,m3:");
marks1=Integer.parseInt(s1.readLine());
marks2=Integer.parseInt(s1.readLine());
marks3=Integer.parseInt(s1.readLine());
avg = (marks1+marks2+marks3)/3;
System.out.println("Roll number is="+rollno);
System.out.println("Average is="+avg);
}
}
```

Output:
C:\cc>java cc2
Enter roll number: 07
Enter marks m1, m2,m3:
66
77
88
Roll number is=7
Average is=77.0

2. 2 MIXING DATA TYPES:

Java allows mixing of constants and variables of different types in an expression, but during assessment it hold to very strict rules of type conversion.

When computer consider operand and operator and if operands are different types then type is automatically convert in higher type.

Following table shows the automatic type conversion.

	char	byte	short	int	long	float	double
Char	int	int	int	int	long	float	double
Byte	int	int	int	int	long	float	double
Short	int	int	int	int	long	float	double
Int	int	int	int	int	long	float	double
Long	long	long	long	long	long	float	double
Float	float	float	float	float	float	float	double
double	double	double	double	double	double	double	double

2.3 VARIABLES:

Variables are labels that express a particular position in memory and connect it with a data type.

The first way to declare a variable: This specifies its data type, and reserves memory for it. It assigns zero to primitive types and null to objects.

dataType variableName;

The second way to declare a variable: This specifies its data type, reserves memory for it, and puts an initial value into that memory. The initial value must be of the correct data type.

dataType variableName = initialValue;
      The first way to declare two variables: all of the same data type, reserves memory for each.

dataType variableNameOne, variableNameTwo;
      The second way to declare two variables: both of the same data type, reserves memory, and puts an initial value in each variable.

dataType variableNameI = initialValueI, variableNameII=initialValueII;

2.3.1 Variable name:

- Use only the characters 'a' through 'z', 'A' through 'Z', '0' through '9', character '_', and character '$'.
- A name cannot include the space character.
- Do not begin with a digit.
- A name can be of any realistic length.
- Upper and lower case count as different characters.
- A name cannot be a reserved word (keyword).
- A name must not previously be in utilized in this block of the program.

CONSTANT :

Constant means fixed value which is not change at the time of execution of program. In Java, there are two types of constant as follows:
    Numeric Constants
        Integer constant
        Real constant
    Character Constants
        Character constant
        String constant

Integer Constant:
An Integer constant refers to a series of digits. There are
three types of integer as follows:
    Decimal integer
        Embedded spaces, commas and characters are not alloed in between digits.
        For example: 23 411
        7,00,000 17.33
    Octal integer
        It allows us any sequence of numbers or digits from 0 to 7 with leading 0 and it is called as Octal integer.
        For example:
        011
        00
        0425
    Hexadecimal integer
It allows the sequence which is preceded by 0X or 0x and it also allows alphabets from 'A' to 'F' or 'a' to 'f' ('A' to 'F' stands for the numbers '10' to '15') it is called as Hexadecimal integer. For example:
    0x7
    00X

2.4.2 Real Constant
It allows us fractional data and it is also called as folating point constant.
It is used for percentage, height and so on. For example:
0.0234
0.777 -1.23

2.4.3 Character Constant
It allows us single character within pair of single coute. For example:
'A'
'7'
'\'

2.4.4 String Constant
It allows us the series of characters within pair of double coute. For example:
"WELCOME"
"END OF PROGRAM" "BYE ...BYE"
"A"

2.4.5 Symbolic constant:
In Java program, there are many things which is requires repeatedly and if we want to make changes then we have to make these changes in whole program where this variable is used. For this purpose, Java provides 'final' keyword to declare the value of variable as follows:
Syntax:
final type Symbolic_name=value;
For example:
If I want to declare the value of 'PI' then:
final float PI=3.1459
the condition is, Symbolic_name will be in capital letter(it shows the difference between normal variable and symblic name) and do not declare in method.

2.4.6 Backslash character constant:
Java support some special character constant which are given in following table.

Constant	Importance
'\b'	Back space
'\t'	Tab
'\n'	New line
'\\'	Backslash
'\"	Single coute
'\"'	Double coute

2.5 Comments:
A **comment** is a note written to a human reader of a program. The program compiles and runs exactly the same with or without comments. Comments start with the two characters "//" (slash slash). Those characters and everything that follows them on the same line are ignored by the java compiler. everything between the two characters "/*"and the two characters "*/" are unobserved by the compiler. There can be many lines of comments between the "/*" and the "*/".

2.6 3 ways for reading input from the user in the console

Three are different ways for reading input from the user in the command line environment (also known as the "console"). Each way is fairly easy to use and also has its own advantages and drawbacks.

1. Using BufferedReader class

By wrapping the **System.in** (standard input stream) in an **InputStreamReader** which is wrapped in a **BufferedReader**, we can read input from the user in the command line.
Here's an example:

```
BufferedReader reader = new BufferedReader(new
InputStreamReader(System.in));
System.out.print("Enter your name: ");
 String name = reader.readLine();
System.out.println("Your name is: " + name);
```

In the above example, the **readLine()** method reads a line of text from the command line.
Advantages: The input is buffered for efficient reading.
Drawbacks: The wrapping code is hard to remember.

2. Using Scanner class

The main purpose of the **Scanner** class (available since Java 1.5) is to parse primitive types and strings using regular expressions, however it is also can be used to read input from the user in the command line.
Here's an example:

```
Scanner scanner = new Scanner(System.in);
System.out.print("Enter your nationality: ");
String nationality = scanner.nextLine();
 System.out.print("Enter your age: ");
int age = scanner.nextInt();
```

Advantages:

Convenient methods for parsing primitives (nextInt(), nextFloat(), ...) from the tokenized input.

Regular expressions can be used to find tokens.

Drawbacks:

The reading methods are not synchronized.

3. Using Console class

The **Console** class was introduced in Java 1.6, and it has been becoming a preferred way for reading user's input from the command line. In addition, it can be used for reading password-like input without echoing the characters entered by the user; the format string syntax can also be used (like System.out.printf()). Here's an example code snippet:

```
Console console = System.console();
if (console == null)
{
   System.out.println("No console: non-interactive mode!");
   System.exit(0);
}
 System.out.print("Enter your username: ");
String username = console.readLine();
System.out.print("Enter your password: ");
char[] password = console.readPassword();
String passport = console.readLine("Enter your %d (th) passport
number: ", 2);
```

Advantages:

Reading password without echoing the entered characters.

Reading methods are synchronized.

Format string syntax can be used.

Drawbacks:

Does not work in non-interactive environment (such as in an IDE).

Combined Example Program

For your convenient and reference purpose, we combine the above code snippet into a demo program whose source code looks like this:

```
package net.codejava.io;
 import java.io.*;
import java.util.*;
 public class UserInputConsoleDemo {
    public static void main(String[] args) {
      // using InputStreamReader
      try {
         BufferedReader reader = new BufferedReader(new
InputStreamReader(System.in));
         System.out.print("Enter your name: ");
         String name = reader.readLine();
         System.out.println("Your name is: " + name);
      } catch (IOException ioe) {
         ioe.printStackTrace();
      }

      // using Scanner
      Scanner scanner = new Scanner(System.in);
      System.out.print("Enter your nationality: ");
      String nationality = scanner.nextLine();
      System.out.println("Your nationality is: " + nationality);
```

```java
// using Console
Console console = System.console();
if (console == null) {
    System.out.println("No console: not in interactive mode!");
    System.exit(0);
}

System.out.print("Enter your username: ");
String username = console.readLine();

System.out.print("Enter your password: ");
char[] password = console.readPassword();

System.out.println("Thank you!");
System.out.println("Your username is: " + username);
System.out.println("Your password is: " +
String.valueOf(password));

// using Console with formatted prompt
String job = console.readLine("Enter your job: ");

String passport = console.readLine("Enter your %d (th)
passport number: ", 2);

System.out.println("Your job is: " + job);
System.out.println("Your passport number is: " + passport);
    }
}
```

2.7 COMMAND LINE ARGUMENTS:

Command line arguments are parameters that are supplied to the application program at the time of invoking its execution. They must be supplied at the time of its execution following the file name.

In the main () method, the args is confirmed as an array of string known as string objects. Any argument provided in the command line at the time of program execution, are accepted to the array args as its elements. Using index or subscripted entry can access the individual elements of an array. The number of element in the array args can be getting with the length parameter.

For example:
```java
class Add
{
public static void main(String args[])
  {
      int a=Integer.parseInt(args[0]); int
      b=Integer.parseInt(args[1]);
      int c=a+b; System.out.println("Addition is="+c);
  }
```

36

}
output:
c:\javac Add.java
c:\java Add 5 2 7

SUMMARY:

In this unit, we learn the concept of dtata types, variable and constants with example. In constants, we gain knowledge of back slash character constant. Additionaly we study the concept of command line argument and comments which is also essential for us.

3

TOKENS IN JAVA

Unit Structure

3.1 INTRODUCTION:

A Java program is basically a set of classes. A class is defined by a set of declaration statements and methods or functions. Most statements contain expressions, which express the actions carried out on information or data. Smallest indivisual thing in a program are known as tokens. The compiler recognizes them for building up expression and statements.

3.2 TOKENS IN JAVA:

There are five types of token as follows:
1. Literals
2. Identifiers
3. Operators
4. Separators

3.2.1 Literals:

Literals in Java are a sequence of characters (digits, letters and other characters) that characterize constant values to be stored in variables. Java language specifies five major types of literals are as follows:

1. Integer literals
2. Floating point literals
3. Character literals
4. String literals
5. Boolean literals

Identifiers:

Identifiers are programmer-created tokens. They are used for naming classes, methods, variables, objects, labels, packages and interfaces in a program. Java identifiers follow the following rules:

1. They can have alphabets, digits, and the underscore and dollar sign characters.
2. They must not start with a digit.
3. Uppercase and lowercase letters are individual.
4. They can be of any length.

Identifier must be meaningful, easily understandable and descriptive.

For example:

Private and local variables like "length".

Name of public methods and instance variables begin with lowercase letter like "addition"

3.2.3 Keywords:

Keywords are important part of Java. Java language has reserved 50 words as keywords. Keywords have specific meaning in Java. We cannot use them as variable, classes and method. Following table shows keywords.

abstract	char	catch	boolean
default	finally	do	implements
if	long	throw	private
package	static	break	double
this	volatile	import	protected
class	throws	byte	else
float	final	public	transient
native	instanceof	case	extends
int	null	const	new
return	try	for	switch
interface	void	while	synchronized
short	continue	goto	super
assert	const		

3.2.4 Operator:

Java carries a broad range of operators. An operator is symbols that specify operation to be performed may be certain mathematical and logical operation. Operators are used in programs to operate data and variables. They frequently form a part of mathematical or logical expressions.

Categories of operators are as follows:

1. Arithmetic operators
2. Logical operators
3. Relational operators
4. Assignment operators
5. Conditional operators
6. Increment and decrement operators

7. Bit wise operators

Arithmetic operators:

Arithmetic operators are used to make mathematical expressions and the working out as same in algebra. Java provides the fundamental arithmetic operators. These can operate on built in data type of Java.

Following table shows the details of operators.

Operator	Importance/ significance
+	Addition
-	Subtraction
/	Division
*	Multiplication
%	Modulo division or remainder

Now the following programs show the use of arithmetic operators.

"+" operator in Java:
In this program, we have to add two integer numbers and display the result.

```
class AdditionInt
{
  public static void main (String args[])
  {
    int a = 6;
    int b = 3;
    System.out.println("a = " + a);
    System.out.println("b =" + b);
    int c = a + b; System.out.println("Addition = " + c);
  }
}
```

Output: a= 6 b= 3
Addition=9

"-" operator in Java:
```
class SubstractionInt
{
  public static void main (String args[])
  {
    int a = 6; int b = 3;
    System.out.println("a = " + a);
    System.out.println("b =" + b);
    int c = a - b;
    System.out.println("Subtraction= " + c);
}
}
```
Output:
a=6
b=3

Subtraction=3

"*" operator in Java:
```
Class MultiplicationInt
{
  public static void main (String args[])
  {

    int a = 6; int b = 3;
    System.out.println("a = " + a);
    System.out.println("b =" + b);
    int c = a * b; System.out.println("Multiplication= " + c);
}
}
```
Output:
a=6
b=3
Multiplication=18

"/" operator in Java:
```
Class DivisionInt
{
  public static void main (String args[])
  {

    int a = 6; int b = 3;
    System.out.println("a = " + a);
    System.out.println("b =" + b);
    c = a / b; System.out.println("division=" + c);
}
}
```
Output:
a=6
b=3
Division=3

Remainder or modulus operator (%) in Java:
```
Class Remainderoptr
{
  public static void main (String args[])
  {

    int a = 6; int b = 3;
    System.out.println("a = " + a);
    System.out.println("b =" + b);
    c = a % b; System.out.println("remainder=" + c);
}
}
```
Output:
a=6
b=3 Remainder= 0

- When both operands in the expression are integers then the expression is called Integer expression and the opration is called Integer arithmetic.

- When both operands in the expression are real then the expression is called Real expression and the opration is called Real arithmetic.
- When one operand in the expression is integer and other is float then the expression is called Mixed Mode Arithmetic expression and the opration is called Mixed Mode Arithmetic operation.

As we learn the Arithmetic operation on integer data and store data in integer variable. But the following program shows the use of operators with integer data and store data in float variable.

Program: write a program to calculate average of three numbers.

```
class Avg1
{
public static void main(String args[])
{
        int a=3; int b=3; int c=4;
        int avg;
avg=a+b+c;
avg=avg/3;
System.out.println("Avg of three numbers="+avg);
}
}
```

Output:
Avg of three numbers=3

Logical operators:
When we want to form compound conditions by combining two or more relations, then we can use logical operators.
Following table shows the details of operators.

Operators	Importance/ significance
||	Logical – OR
&&	Logical –AND
!	Logical –NOT

The logical expression defer a value of true or false. Following table shows the truth table of Logical – OR and Logical – AND.
Truth table for Logical – OR operator:

Operand1	Operand3	Operand1 || Operand3
T	T	T
T	F	T
F	T	T
F	F	F

T - True

F - False

Truth table for Logical – AND operator:

Operand1	Operand3	Operand1 && Operand3
T	T	T
T	F	F
F	T	F
F	F	F

T – True
F – False
Now the following program shows the use of Logical operators. class LogicalOptr

```
{
 public static void main (String args[])
 {

    boolean a = true; boolean b =
    false;

    System.out.println("a||b = " +(a||b));
    System.out.println("a&&b = "+(a&&b));
    System.out.println("a! = "+(!a));
 }
}
```

Output: a||b = true
a&&b = false a! = false

3.2.4.3 Relational Operators:

When evaluation of two numbers is performed depending upon their relation, assured decisions are made.
The value of relational expression is either true or false.
If A=7 and A < 10 is true while 10 < A is false.
Following table shows the details of operators.

Operator	Importance/ significance
>	Greater than
<	Less than
!=	Not equal to
>=	Greater than or equal to
<=	Less than or equal to

Now, following examples show the actual use of operators.
    If 10 > 30 then result is false
    If 40 > 17 then result is true
    If 10 >= 300 then result is false
    If 10 <= 10 then result is true

Now the following program shows the use of operators.
    Program 1:

43

```java
class Reloptr1
{
  public static void main (String args[])
  {
    int a = 10; int b = 30;
    System.out.println("a>b = " +(a>b));
    System.out.println("a<b = "+(a<b));
    System.out.println("a<=b = "+(a<=b));
  }
}
```
Output: a>b = false a<b = true a<=b = true

Program 2
```java
class Reloptr2
{
  public static void main (String args[])
  {
    int a = 10; int b = 30;
    int c=30;
    System.out.println("a>b = " +(a>b));
    System.out.println("a<b = "+(a<b));
    System.out.println("a<=c = "+(a<=c));
    System.out.println("c>b = " +(c>b));
    System.out.println("a<c = "+(a<c));
    System.out.println("b<=c = "+(b<=c));
  }
}
```

Output:
a>b = false a<b = true a<=c = true c>b = true a<c = true b<=c = true

Assignment Operators:
Assignment Operators is used to assign the value of an expression to a variable and is also called as Shorthand operators. Variable_name binary_operator = expression Following table show the use of assignment operators.

Simple Assignment Operator	Statement with shorthand Operators
A=A+1	A+=1
A=A-1	A-=1
A=A/(B+1)	A/=(B+1)
A=A*(B+1)	A*=(B+1)
A=A/C	A/=C
A=A%C	A%=C

These operators avoid repetition, easier to read and write.
Now the following program shows the use of operators.
```java
class Assoptr
{
  public static void main (String args[])
  {
```

```
int a = 10; int b = 30;
int c = 30; a+=1; b-=3;
c*=7;
System.out.println("a = " +a);
System.out.println("b = "+b);
System.out.println("c = "+c);
  }
}
```
Output: a = 11 b = 18 c=310

3.2.4.5 Conditional Operators:

The character pair ?: is a ternary operator of Java, which is used to construct conditional expressions of the following form:

Expression1 ? Expression3 : Expression3

The operator ? : works as follows:

Expression1 is evaluated if it is true then Expression3 is evaluated and becomes the value of the conditional expression. If Expression1 is false then Expression3 is evaluated and its value becomes the conditional expression.

For example:
A=3;
B=4;
C=(A<B)?A:B;
C=(3<4)?3:4;
C=4

Now the following program shows the use of operators.
```
class Coptr
{
  public static void main (String args[])
  {
    int a = 10; int b = 30; int c;
    c=(a>b)?a:b; System.out.println("c = " +c);
     c=(a<b)?a:b; System.out.println("c = " +c);
  }
}
```
Output: c = 30 c = 10

program3: Write a program to check whether number is positive or negative.
```
class PosNeg
{
        public static void main(String args[])
        {
        int a=10;
        int flag=(a<0)?0:1; if(flag==1)
                System.out.println("Number is positive");
        else
                System.out.println("Number is negative");
        }
```

}Output:
Number is positive

3.2.4.6 Increment and Decrement Operators:
The increment operator ++ adds 1 to a variable. Usually the variable is an integer type, but it can be a floating point type. The two plus signs must not be split by any character. Usually they are written immediately next to the variable.
Following table shows the use of operators.

Expression	Process	Example	end result
A++	Add 1 to a variable after use.	int A=10,B; B=A++;	A=11 B=10
++A	Add 1 to a variable before use.	int A=10,B; B=++A;	A=11 B=11
A--	Subtract 1 from a variable after use.	int A=10,B; B=A--;	A=9 B=10
--A	Subtract 1 from a variable before use.	int A=10,B; B=--A;	A=9 B=9

Now the following program shows the use of operators.

```
class IncDecOp
{
public static void main(String args[])
{
int x=1; int y=3; int u;
int z; u=++y; z=x++;
System.out.println(x);
System.out.println(y);
System.out.println(u);
System.out.println(z);
}
}
```

Output:
3
4
4
1

Bit Wise Operators:
Bit wise operator execute single bit of their operands. Following table shows bit wise operator:

Operator	Importance/ significance
		Bitwise OR
&	Bitwise AND
&=	Bitwise AND assignment
|=	Bitwise OR assignment
^	Bitwise Exclusive OR
<<	Left shift
>>	Right shift
~	One's complement

Now the following program shows the use of operators.

Program 1

```
class Boptr1
{
  public static void main (String args[])
  {
    int a = 4;
    int b = a<<3;
        System.out.println("a = " +a);
        System.out.println("b = " +b);
  }
}
```

Output:
=4
=16

Program 2

```
Class Boptr2
{
public static void main (String args[])
  {
    int a = 16; int b = a>>3;
    System.out.println("a = " +a);
    System.out.println("b = " +b);
  }
}
```
Output: a = 16 b = 3

Separator:

Separators are symbols. It shows the separated code.they describe function of our code.

Name	Use
()	Parameter in method definition, containing statements for conditions,etc.
{}	It is used for define a code for method and classes
[]	It is used for declaration of array
;	It is used to show the separate statement
,	It is used to show the separation in identifier in variable Declarartion
.	It is used to show the separate package name from sub-packages and classes, separate variable and method from reference variable.

3.3 OPERATOR PRECEDENCE IN JAVA:

An arithmetic expression without any parentheses will be calculated from left to right using the rules of precedence of operators.

There are two priority levels of arithmetic operators are as follows:

High priority (* / %)
Low priority (+ -)

The evaluation process includes two left to right passes through the expression. During the first pass, the high priority operators are applied as they are encountered.

During the second pass, the low priority operators are applied as they are encountered.

For example:

Z=A-B/3+C*3-1
When A=10, B=13, C=3
First pass:
Z=10-(13/3) + (3*3)-1
Z=10-4+3-1
Second pass:
Z=6+3-1
Z=7
Answer is=7

Following table shows associativity of operators.

Operator	Associativity	Rank
[ ]	Left to right	1
( )	Left to right	
.	Left to right	
-	Right to left	
++	Right to left	3
--	Right to left	
!	Right to left	
~	Right to left	
(type)	Right to left	
*	Left to right	3
/	Left to right	
%	Left to right	
+	Left to right	4
-	Left to right	
<<	Left to right	5
>>	Left to right	
>>>	Left to right	
<	Left to right	
<=	Left to right	6
>	Left to right	

>=	Left to right	
Instanceof	Left to right	
==	Left to right	7
!=	Left to right	
&	Left to right	8
^	Left to right	9
|	Left to right	10
&&	Left to right	11
||	Left to right	13
?:	Right to left	13
=	Right to left	14

SUMMARY:

In this unit, we learn the cocept of tokens in java.There are 4 types of tokens as we learn:

Literals
Identifiers
Operators
Types of operators are:
Arithmetic operators
Logical operators
Relational operators
Assignment operators
Conditional operators
Increment and decrement operators
Bit wise operator

We learn these operators with example.

separator

4

CONTROL STRUCTURE

4.1 INTRODUCTION:

In Java, program is a set of statements and which are executed sequentially in order in which they appear. In that statements, some calculation have need of executing with some conditions and for that we have to provide control to that statements. In other words, Control statements are used to provide the flow of execution with condition.

In this unit, we will learn the control structure in detail.

4.2 CONTROL STRUCTURE:

In java program, control structure is can divide in three parts:

Selection statement
Iteration statement
Jumps in statement

4.2.1 Selection Statement:

Selection statement is also called as Decision making statements because it provides the decision making capabilities to the statements.

In selection statement, there are two types:

if statement

switch statement

These two statements are allows you to control the flow of a program with their conditions.

4.2.1.1 if Statement:

The "if statement" is also called as conditional branch statement. It is used to program execution through two paths. The syntax of "if statement" is as follows:

Syntax:

```
if (condition)
{
Statement 1;
Statement 2;
...
}
else
{
Statement 3;
Statement 4;
...
}
```

The "if statement" is a commanding decision making statement and is used to manage the flow of execution of statements. The "if statement" is the simplest one in decision statements. Above syntax is shows two ways decision statement and is used in combination with statements.
Following figure shows the "if statement"

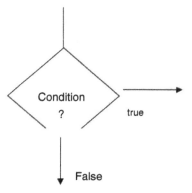

4.2.1.1.1 Simple if statement:
Syntax:
```
If (condition)
{
Statement block;
}
Statement-a;
```

In statement block, there may be single statement or multiple statements. If the condition is true then statement block will be executed. If the condition is false then statement block will omit and statement-a will be executed.

4.2.1.1.2 The if…else statement:

Syntax:
If (condition)
```
        {
                True - Statement block;
        }
else
        {
                False - Statement block;
        }
        Statement-a;
```

If the condition is true then True - statement block will be executed. If the condition is false then False - statement block will be executed. In both cases the statement-a will always executed.

Following program shows the use of if statement.
   Program: write a program to check whether the number is positive or negative.

```
import java.io.*;
class NumTest
{
        public static void main (String[] args) throws IOException
        {
                int Result=11; System.out.println("Number
                is"+Result);
                                if ( Result < 0 )

                {System.out.println("The number "+ Result +" is negative");
        }
                else
                {
        System.out.println("The number "+ Result +" is positive");
                }
        System.out.println("------- * ---------");
        }
}
```

Output:
C:\MCA>java NumTest
Number is 11
The number 11 is positive

(All conditional statements in Java require boolean values, and that's what the ==, <, >, <=, and >= operators all return. A boolean is a value that is either true or false. If you need to set a boolean variable in a Java program, you have to use the constants true and false. Boolean values are no more integers than are strings).

For example: write a program to check whether the number is divisible by 2 or not.

```java
import java.io.*;
class divisorDemo
{
public static void main(String[ ] args)
{
      int a =11;
      if(a%2==0)
      {
          System.out.println(a +" is divisible by 2");
      }
      else
      {
          System.out.println(a+" is not divisible by 2");
      }
}
}
```

Output:
C:\MCA>java divisorDemo

11 is not divisible by 2

4.2.1.1.3 Nesting of if-else statement:
Syntax:
```
if (condition1)
        {
        If(condition2)
            {
                    Statement block1;
            }
        else
            {
                    Statement block2;
            }
        }
        else
        {
                    Statement block3;
        }
        Statement 4:
```

If the condition1 is true then it will be goes for condition2. If the condition2 is true then statement block1 will be executed otherwise statement2 will be executed. If the condition1 is false then statement block3 will be executed. In both cases the statement4 will always executed.

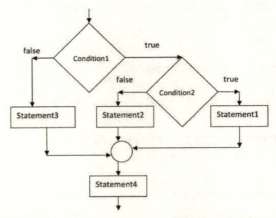

For example: Write a program to find out greatest number from three numbers.

```
class greatest
    {
    public static void main (String args[ ])
            {
                int a=10;
                int b=20;
                int c=3;

                if(a>b)

                    {
                       if(a>c)
                       {
                            System.out.println("a is greater number");
                       }
                       else
                       {
                            System.out.println("c is greater number");
                       }

                    }
                else
                    {
                       if(c>b)
                       {
                            System.out.println("c is greater number");
                       }
                       else
                       {
                            System.out.println("b is greater number");
                       }
                    }
            }
    }
```

Output:
C:\MCA>java greatest

b is greater number

4.2.1.2 switch statement:
In Java, switch statement check the value of given variable or statement against a list of case values and when the match is found a statement-block of that case is executed. Switch statement is also called as multiway decision statement.
Syntax:
switch(condition)// condition means case value
{
       case value-1:statement block1;break;
       case value-2:statement block2;break;
       case value-3:statement block3;break;
       …
       default:statement block-default;break;
}
statement a;

The condition is byte, short, character or an integer. value-1,value-2,value-3,…are constant and is called as labels. Each of these values be matchless or unique with the statement. Statement block1, Statement block2, Statement block3,..are list of statements which contain one statement or more than one statements. Case label is always end with ":" (colon).

Program: write a program for bank account to perform following operations.
   -Check balance
   -withdraw amount
   -deposit amount

For example:
```
import java.io.*;
class bankac
    {
    public static void main(String args[]) throws Exception
    int bal=20000;
    int ch=Integer.parseInt(args[0]);
    System.out.println("Menu");
    System.out.println("1:check balance");
    System.out.println("2:withdraw amount... plz enter choice and amount");
    System.out.println("3:deposit amount... plz enter choice and amount");
    System.out.println("4:exit");
    switch(ch)
    {
    case 1:
    System.out.println("Balance is:"+bal);
    break;
    case 2:
    int w=Integer.parseInt(args[1]);
```

```java
        if(w>bal)
            {
            System.out.println("Not sufficient balance");
            }
            bal=bal-w; System.out.println("Balance is"+bal); break;
        case 3:
            int d=Integer.parseInt(args[1]); bal=bal+d;
            System.out.println("Balance is"+bal); break;
        default:
            break;
        }
    }
}
```

Output:
C:\MCA>javac bankac.java
C:\MCA>java bankac 1 Menu
1:check balance
2:withdraw amount... plz enter choice and amount
3:deposit amount... plz enter choice and amount
4:exit
Balance is:20000

C:\MCA>java bankac 2 2000 Menu
1:check balance
2:withdraw amount... plz enter choice and amount
3:deposit amount... plz enter choice and amount
4:exit
Balance is18000

C:\MCA>java bankac 3 2000 Menu
1:check balance
2:withdraw amount... plz enter choice and amount
3:deposit amount... plz enter choice and amount
4:exit
Balance is 22000

C:\MCA>java bankac 4
Menu
1:check balance
2:withdraw amount... plz enter choice and amount
3:deposit amount... plz enter choice and amount
4:exit

C:\MCA>java bankac

4.2.2 Iteration Statement:

The process of repeatedly executing a statements and is called as looping. The statements may be executed multiple times (from zero to infinite number). If a loop executing continuous then it is called as Infinite loop. Looping is also called as iterations.

In Iteration statement, there are three types of operation:
   for loop
   while loop
   do-while loop

4.2.2.1 for loop:
        The for loop is entry controlled loop. It means that it provide a more concious loop control structure.

Syntax:
for(initialization;condition;iteration)

//iteration means increment/ decrement

{
Statement block;
}
When the loop is starts, first part(i.e. initialization) is execute. It is just like a counter and provides the initial value of loop. But the thing is, I nitialization is executed only once. The next part(i.e. condition) is executed after the initialization. The important thing is, this part provide the condition for looping. If the condition will satisfying then loop will execute otherwise it will terminate.

Third part(i.e. iteration) is executed after the condition. The statements that incremented or decremented the loop control variables.

For example:
```
import java.io.*;
class number
{
public static void main(String args[]) throws Exception
{
int i;
System.out.println("list of 1 to 10 numbers");
for(i=1;i<=10;i++)
{
System.out.println(i);
}
}
}
```
Output:
C:\MCA>javac number.java
C:\MCA>java number
list of 1 to 10 numbers
1
2
3
4
5
6
7
8
9
10

Here we declare i=1 and then it check the condition that if i<10 then only loop will be executed. After first iteration the value of i will print and it will incremented by 1. Now the value of i=2 and again we have to check the condition and value of i will print and then increment I by 1 and so on.

4.2.2.2 while loop:
The while loop is entry controlled loop statement. The condition is evaluated, if the condition is true then the block of statements or statement block is executed otherwise the block of statement is not executed.

Syntax:
While(condition)
{
Statement block;
}

For example: Write a program to display 1 to 10 numbers using while loop.

```
import java.io.*;
class number
{
public static void main(String args[]) throws Exception
{
int i=1;
System.out.println("list of 1 to 10 numbers");
while(i<=10)
{
System.out.println(i);
i++;
}
}
}
```

Output:
C:\MCA>javac number.java
C:\MCA>java number
list of 1 to 10 numbers 1 2 3 4 5 6 7 8 9 10

4.2.2.3 do-while loop:
In do-while loop, first attempt of loop should be execute then it check the condition.

The benefit of do-while loop/statement is that we get entry in loop and then condition will check for very first time. In while loop, condition will check first and if condition will not satisfied then the loop will not execute.

Syntax:
do
{
Statement block;
}

While(condition);

In program,when we use the do-while loop, then in very first attempt, it allows us to get enter in loop and execute that loop and then check the condition.
Following program show the use of do-while loop.
For example: Write a program to display 1 to 10 numbers using do-while loop.

```
import java.io.*;
class number
{
    public static void main(String args[]) throws Exception
    {
      int i=1;
      System.out.println("list of 1 to 10 numbers");
      do
      {
           System.out.println(i);
           i++;
      }while(i<=10);
    }
}
```

Output:
list of 1 to 10 numbers
1
2
3
4
5
6
7
8
9
10

4.2.3 Jumps in statement:
Statements or loops perform a set of operartions continually until the control variable will not satisfy the condition. but if we want to break the loop when condition will satisy then Java give a permission to jump from one statement to end of loop or beginning of loop as well as jump out of a loop.
"break" keyword use for exiting from loop and "continue" keyword use for continuing the loop.
Following statements shows the exiting from loop by using "break" statement.

do-while loop:
```
do
{
.................

.................
```

```
if(condition)
{
break;//exit from if loop and do-while loop
}
……………..
……………..
}
While(condition);
………..
………..
```

For loop:
```
for(…………)
{
……………
…………..

if(…………..)

break; ;//exit from if loop and for loop
……………
……………
}
……………
…………..
```

While loop:
```
while(…………)
{
……………
…………..
if(…………..)
break; ;//exit from if loop and while loop
……………
……………
}
```

Following statements shows the continuing the loop by using "continue" statement.

do-while loop:
```
do
{
………………
………………
if(condition)
{
continue;//continue the do-while loop
}
……………..
……………..
}
```

While(condition);
………..
………..

For loop:
```
for(…………)
{
……………
……………
if(…………..)
continue ;// continue the for loop
……………
……………
}
……………
……………
```
While loop:
```
while(…………)
{
……………
……………
if(…………..)
continue ;// continue the while loop
……………
……………
}
……………
……………
```
Labelled loop:
We can give label to a block of statements with any valid name.following example shows the use of label, break and continue.

For example:
```
Import java.io.*; class Demo
   {
   public static void main(String args[]) throws Exception
          {
          int j,i;
          LOOP1: for(i=1;i<100;i++)
                 {
                        System.out.println("");
                        if(i>=10)
                           {
                           break;
                           }
                        for(j=1;j<100;j++)
                           {
                                System.out.println("$ "); if(i==j)

                                {
                                        continue LOOP1;
```

```
                        }
                 }

              }
        System.out.println(" End of program ");
        }
}
```
Output:
```
$
$ $
$ $ $
$ $ $ $
$ $ $ $ $
$ $ $ $ $ $
$ $ $ $ $ $ $
$ $ $ $ $ $ $ $
$ $ $ $ $ $ $ $ $
```

End of program

SUMMARY:

In this unit, we covered Selection Statement, Iteration Statement and Jump in Statement. In Selection statement, we covered if statement and switch statement with example. In Iteration Statement, we covered for loop, while loop and do-while loop with example. In Jump in Statement, we covered break, continue and label with example.

5

CLASSES

Unit Structure

Objective

class

Creating "main" in a separate class

Methods with parameters

Methods with a Return Type

Method Overloading

Passing Objects as Parameters

Passing Values to methods and Constructor:

Abstract Classes

Extending the class:

Summary:

5.1 OBJECTIVE :

In this lesson of Java Tutorial, you will learn...

How to create class

How to create method

How to create constructor

CLASS

Definition: A class is a collection of objects of similar type. Once a class is defined, any number of objects can be produced which belong to that class.

Class Declaration

```
class classname
{
...
ClassBody
...
}
```

Objects are instances of the Class. Classes and Objects are very much related to each other. Without objects you can't use a class.

A general class declaration:

```
class name1
{
//public variable declaration void
methodname()
{
//body of method... //Anything
```

```
}
}
```
Now following example shows the use of method.
```
class Demo
{
private int x,y,z;
public void input()
{
x=10;
y=15;
}
public void sum()
{
z=x+y;
}
public void print_data()
{
System.out.println("Answer is =" +z);
}
public static void main(String args[])
{
Demo object=new Demo(); object.input();
object.sum(); object.print_data();
}
}
```

In program,
```
Demo object=new Demo(); object.input();
object.sum(); object.print_data();
```

In the first line we created an object.

The three methods are called by using the dot operator. When we call a method the code inside its block is executed.

The dot operator is used to call methods or access them.

5.2.1 Creating "main" in a separate class

We can create the main method in a separate class, but during compilation you need to make sure that you compile the class with the "main" method.
```
class Demo
{
private int x,y,z; public void input()
{
x=10;
y=15;
}
```

```
public void sum()
{
z=x+y;
}
public void print_data()
{
System.out.println("Answer is =" +z);
}
}

class SumDemo
{
public static void main(String args[])
{
Demo object=new Demo(); object.input();
object.sum(); object.print_data();
}
}
```

Use of dot operator

We can access the variables by using dot operator. Following program shows the use of dot operator.

```
class DotDemo
{
int x,y,z;
public void sum()
{
 z=x+y;
}
    public void show(){ System.out.println("The Answer is "+z);
}
}

class Demo1
{
public static void main(String args[])
{
DotDemo object=new DotDemo();
DotDemo object2=new DotDemo();
object.x=10;
object.y=15;
object2.x=5;
object2.y=10;
object.sum();
```

```
object.show();
object2.sum();
object2.show();
}
}
```

output :
```
C:\cc>javac Demo1.java
C:\cc>java Demo1
The Answer is 25
The Answer is 15
```

Instance Variable

All variables are also known as instance variable. This is because of the fact that each instance or object has its own copy of values for the variables. Hence other use of the *"dot"* operator is to initialize the value of variable for that instance.

5.2.2 Methods with parameters

Following program shows the method with passing parameter.

```
class prg
{
int n,n2,sum;
public void take(int x,int y)
{
n=x;
n2=y;
}
public void sum()
{
sum=n+n2;
}
public void print()
{
System.out.println("The Sum is"+sum);
}
}
class prg1
{
public static void main(String args[])
{
prg obj=new prg();
obj.take(10,15);
obj.sum(); obj.print();
}
}
```

5.2.3 Methods with a Return Type

When method return some value that is the type of that method.

For Example: some methods are with parameter but that method did not return any value that means type of method is void. And if method return integer value then the type of method is an integer.

Following program shows the method with their return type.

```
class Demo1
{
int n,n2;
public void take( int x,int y)
{
n=x;
n=y;
}
public int process()
{
return (n+n2);
}
}

class prg
{
public static void main(String args[])
{
int sum;
Demo1 obj=new Demo1();
obj.take(15,25);
sum=obj.process();
System.out.println("The sum is"+sum);
}
}
```

Output:

The sum is25

5.2.4 Method Overloading

Method overloading means method name will be same but each method should be different parameter list.

```
class prg1
{
```

```java
int x=5,y=5,z=0; public void
sum()
{
z=x+y; System.out.println("Sum is "+z);
}
public void sum(int a,int b)
{
x=a;
y=b;
z=x+y; System.out.println("Sum is "+z);
}
public int sum(int a)
{
x=a;
z=x+y; return z;
}
}

class Demo
{
public static void main(String args[])
{
prg1 obj=new prg1();
obj.sum();
obj.sum(10,12);
System.out.println(+obj.sum(15));
}
}
```
Output:
sum is 10
sum is 22 27

Passing Objects as Parameters
Objects can even be passed as parameters.
```java
class para123
{
int n,n2,sum,mul;
public void take(int x,int y)
{
n=x;
n2=y;
}
public void sum()
```

```
{
sum=n+n2;
System.out.println("The Sum is"+sum);
}
public void take2(para123 obj)
{
n=obj.n;
n2=obj.n2;
}
public void multi()
{
mul=n*n2;
System.out.println("Product is"+mul);
}
}
class DemoPara
{
public static void main(String args[])
{
para123 ob=new para123();
ob.take(3,7);
ob.sum();
ob.take2(ob);
ob.multi();
}
}
```

Output:
C:\cc>javac DemoPara.java
C:\cc>java DemoPara
The Sum is10
Product is21

We have defined a method *"take2"* that declares an object named obj as parameter. We have passed ob to our method. The method *"take2"* automatically gets 3,7 as values for n and n2.

5.2.6 Passing Values to methods and Constructor:

These are two different ways of supplying values to methods.

Classified under these two titles –

1.Pass by Value

2.Pass by Address or Reference

Pass by Value-When we pass a data type like int, float or any other datatype to a method or some constant values like(15,10). They are all passed by value. A copy of variable's value is passed to the receiving method and hence any changes made to the values do not affect the actual variables.

```
class Demopbv
{
int n,n2;
public void get(int x,int y)
{
x=x*x; //Changing the values of passed arguments y=y*y;
//Changing the values of passed arguments
}
}
class Demo345
{
public static void main(String args[])
{
int a,b; a=1; b=2;
System.out.println("Initial Values of a & b "+a+" "+b);
Demopbv obj=new Demopbv();
obj.get(a,b);
System.out.println("Final Values "+a+" "+b);
}
}
Output:
 C:\cc>javac Demo345.java
C:\cc>java Demo345
Initial Values of a & b 1 2
Final Values 1 2
```

Pass by Reference

Objects are always passed by reference. When we pass a value by reference, the reference or the memory address of the variables is passed. Thus any changes made to the argument causes a change in the values which we pass.

Demonstrating Pass by Reference---

```
class pass_by_ref
{
int n,n2;
public void get(int a,int b)
{
n=a;
n2=b;
}
public void doubleit(pass_by_ref temp)
```

```
{
temp.n=temp.n*2;
temp.n2=temp.n2*2;
}
}
class apply7
{
public static void main(String args[])
{
int x=5,y=10;
pass_by_ref obj=new pass_by_ref();
obj.get(x,y);
```
//Pass by Value
```
System.out.println("Initial Values are-- ");
System.out.println(+obj.n);
System.out.println(+obj.n2);
obj.doubleit(obj);
```
//Pass by Reference
```
System.out.println("Final Values are");
System.out.println(+obj.n);
System.out.println(+obj.n2);
}
}
```

5.2.7 Abstract Classes
Definition: An abstract class is a class that is declared as abstract. It may or may not include abstract methods. Abstract classes cannot be instantiated, but they can be subclass.

An abstract method is a method that is declared without an implementation (without braces, and followed by a semicolon), like this:

abstract void studtest(int rollno, double testfees);

If a class includes abstract methods, the class itself must be declared abstract, as in:

public abstract class GraphicObject
{
  declare fields
  declare non-abstract methods abstract void

  draw();

}

When an abstract class is subclass, the subclass usually provides implementations for all of the abstract methods in its parent class. However, if it does not, the subclass must also be declared abstract.

For example: In an object-oriented drawing application, you can draw circles, rectangles, lines, Bezier curves, and many other graphic objects. These objects all have certain states (for example: position, orientation, line color, fill color) and behaviors (for example: moveTo, rotate, resize, draw) in common. Some of these states and behaviors are the same for all graphic objects—for example: position, fill color, and moveTo. Others require different implementations—for example, resize or draw. All GraphicObjects must know how to draw or resize themselves; they just differ in how they do it. This is a perfect situation for an abstract superclass. You can take advantage of the similarities and declare all the graphic objects to inherit from the same abstract parent object—for example, GraphicObject, as shown in the following figure.

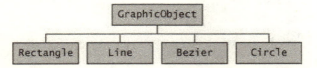

How to implement above diagram concept with source code:
```
abstract class GraphicObject
{
    int x, y;
    ...
    void moveTo(int newX, int newY)
    {
        ...
    }
    abstract void draw();
    abstract void resize();
}
```

Each non-abstract subclass of GraphicObject, such as Circle and Rectangle, must provide implementations for the draw and resize methods:
```
class Circle extends GraphicObject {
    void draw() {
        ...
    }
    void resize() {
        ...
    }
}
```

```
class Rectangle extends GraphicObject {
    void draw() {
        ...
    }
    void resize() {
```

```
...
    }
}
```

Abstract classes are those which can be used for creation of objects. However their methods and constructors can be used by the child or extended class. The need for abstract classes is that you can generalize the super class from which child classes can share its methods. The subclass of an abstract class which can create an object is called as "concrete class".

For example:
```
Abstract class A
{
abstract void method1();
void method2()
{
System.out.println("this is real method");
}
}

class B extends A
{
void method1()
{
System.out.println("B is execution of method1");
}
}

class demo
{
public static void main(String arg[])
{
B  b=new  B();  b.method1();
b.method2();
}
}
```

5.2.8 Extending the class:
Inheritance allows to subclass or child class to access all methods and variables of parent class.
Syntax:
```
class subclassname extends superclassname
{
Varables;
Methods;
.....
}
```
For example: calculate area and volume by using Inhertance. class data

```java
{
int l; int b;
data(int c, int d)
{
l=c;
b=d;
}
int area( )
{
return(l*b);
}
}
class data2 extends data
{
int h;
data2(int c,int d, int a)
{
super(c,d);
h=a;
}
int volume()
{
return(l*b*h);
}
}
class dataDemo
{
public static void main(String args[])
{
data2 d1=new data2(10,20,30);
int area1=d1.area(); //superclass method int
volume1=d1.volume( );// subclass method
System.out.println("Area="+area1);
System.out.println("Volume="+volume1);
}
}
```

Output:
C:\cc>javac dataDemo.java
C:\cc>java dataDemo
Area=200
Volume=6000

"Is A" - is a subclass of a superclass (ex: extends) "Has A" - has a reference to (ex: variable, ref to object).

- o **Access Control** –

Away to limit the access others have to your code.

- **Same package** - can access each others' variables and methods, except for private members.
- **Outside package** - can access public classes. Next, can access members that are public. Also, can access protected members if the class is a subclass of that class.

Same package - use package keyword in first line of source file, or no package keyword and in same directory.

- o **Keywords -**

public - outside of package access.

[no keyword] default - same package access only.

protected - same package access. Access if class is a subclass of, even if in another package.

private - same class access only.

SUMMARY:

In this unit, we learn the concept of class and how to create method and how to pass parameters by value and by reference and method overloading with example.

6

INTERFACES

Unit Structure
Introduction
More about 'interface'
Access
Multiple Inheritance
Interfaces and Abstract Classes
Inheritance within interfaces
Summary

6.1 INTRODUCTION
In chapter 5 you have learnt the following concepts:

> **Abstract** class, which allows you to create methods in a class without writing the code for execution of the method (implementation of the method).

> **Inheritance** through the keyword **'extends'** which tells the machine that an (inherited) class defined is of the type of a base class.

> Methods in the inherited class must provide implementation. (except when the inherited class is an **Abstract** class as well.

Interface takes the above concepts even further. It provides a mechanism to define a class with absolutely no implementation (code for execution of a method or logic).

6.2 MORE ABOUT 'INTERFACE'
One or more classes can **implement** a defined **interface**

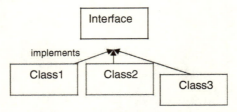

When a class implements a defined interface, it has to implement (write the code, execution logic) for all the methods defined by the interface. The class is free to define more methods if necessary.

e.g.

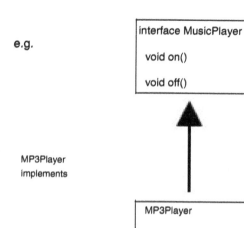

MP3Player
implements

In this example, class MP3Player implements interface MusicPlayer. Here all methods of MusicPlayer are implemented; and there is one more additional method "addMusic()"

Similarly, you could have other classes inherit from the same interface MusicPlayer. Examples –

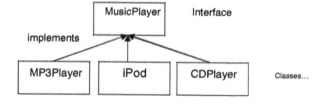

Syntax of Interface

To define an interface, use the **interface** keyword instead of the **class** keyword.
SYNTAX: package xxx.xxx;

interface MusicPlayer
{
   // Cannot have method implementations:

void on();

void off();

void play();

void stop();

}

Points to note above:
   A semicolon after the method definition
   No implementation logic in the method above
   interface keyword instead of class

6.3 ACCESS

In the above example, we've not defined whether the interface is public, private or protected. A private interface makes no sense. If not defined the above interface is visible in the package where the interface belongs. You can define an interface public – which means the interface is visible outside the package as well.

Methods inside the interface are public by default. So in the above example, the methods are public and visible outside of the package as well.

The class which inherits the methods must explicitly define the methods to be public.

SYNTAX:
class MP3Player implements MusicPlayer
{
public void on()
{
        System.out.println("the MP3 Player is ON");

}
public void off()
{
        System.out.println("the MP3 Player is OFF");
}
public void play()
{

        System.out.println("the MP3 Player is playing");

```
}
public void stop()
{
        System.out.println("the MP3 Player is off");
}
}
```

6.4 MULTIPLE INHERITANCE

In Java, there is nothing which prevents from inheriting from multiple interfaces. Since there are no implementations in the methods (code in the methods), there is no danger or overwriting any implementations between multiple interfaces.

```
// Multiple interfaces.
interface MusicPlayer
{
void on();
void off();
void play();
void stop();
}
}

interface VideoPlayer

{

void on();

void off(); void play(); void stop();

void changeContrast(int x); void changeBrightness(int x);

}
}


class iPod implements MusicPlayer, VideoPlayer{ public void on(){

        System.out.println("the MP3 Player is ON");

}
public void off()
{

        System.out.println("the MP3 Player is OFF");
}
public void play(){
                System.out.println("the MP3 Player is playing");
}
```

```java
public void stop(){
        System.out.println("the MP3 Player is off");
}
public void changeContrast(int x){ System.out.println("Constrast

        Changed by" + x);

}
public void changeBrightness(int x){ System.out.println("Brightnesss

        Changed by" + x);

}
}
```

6.5 INTERFACES AND ABSTRACT CLASSES

Interfaces are similar to abstract classes. The differences are as follows:

- All methods in an interface are abstract. Which means all methods must be empty; no code implemented.

- In abstract class, the methods can have code/implementation within it. Atleast one method must be abstract.

- All properties (data fields) in an interface are static final. Properties in an abstract class need not be static final.

- Interfaces are implemented(implements keyword); Abstract classes are extended(extends keyword)

- Class can extend only one abstract class; where as a class can implement multiple interfaces (multiple inheritance)

- Contractual obligation: When a class specifies that it implements an interface, it must define all methods of that interface. A class can implement many different interfaces. If a class doesn't define all methods of the interfaces it agreed to define (by the implements clause), the compiler gives an error message, which typically says something like "This class must be declared abstract". An abstract class is one that doesn't implement all methods it said it would. The solution to this is almost always to implement the missing methods of the interface. A misspelled method name or incorrect parameter list is the usual cause, not that it should have been abstract!

6.6 INHERITANCE WITHIN INTERFACES

You can add new methods to an existing interface by extending it; and adding new methods.

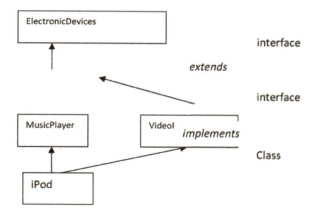

In the above example, please note
    ElectronicDevices is an interface.
    MusicPlayer and VideoPlayer are interfaces which "**extend**" ElectronicDevices
    iPod is a class which implements MusicPlayer and VideoPlayer

So, if ElectronicDevices interface had one property – which is "powerSource"; it would be inherited by all classes which implement MusicPlayer or VideoPlayer

Example for practice:

        Write a class that implements the CharSequence interface found in the java.lang package. Your implementation should return the string backwards. Select one of the sentences from this book to use as the data. Write a small main method to test your class; make sure to call all four methods.

Answer 1:
```
// CharSequenceDemo presents a String value -- backwards.
public class CharSequenceDemo implements CharSequence
{
    private String s;
    public CharSequenceDemo(String s)
    {
    //It would be much more efficient to just reverse the string //in the constructor.
    this.s = s;
}
private int fromEnd(int i) { return s.length() - 1
    - i;

}
```

81

```java
public char charAt(int i)
{
    if ((i < 0) || (i >= s.length())))
    {
        throw new StringIndexOutOfBoundsException(i);
    }
    return s.charAt(fromEnd(i));
}

public int length()
{
return s.length();
}

public CharSequence subSequence(int start, int end) { if (start < 0)
{
        throw new StringIndexOutOfBoundsException(start);
}

    if (end > s.length()) {
        throw new StringIndexOutOfBoundsException(end);
    }

    if (start > end) {
        throw new StringIndexOutOfBoundsException(start - end);
        }
        StringBuilder sub =
        new StringBuilder(s.subSequence (from End(end),from End (start)));
        return sub.reverse();
    }

    public String toString() {
        StringBuilder s = new StringBuilder(this.s); return
        s.reverse().toString();
    }

    //Random int from 0 to max. private static int
    random(int max) {
        return (int) Math.round(Math.random() * max + 0.5);
    }

    public static void main(String[] args) {
        CharSequenceDemo s =
        new CharSequenceDemo("Write a class that implements the CharSequence
interface found in the java.lang package.");
        //exercise charAt() and length() for (int i = 0; i <
        s.length(); i++) {
            System.out.println(s.charAt(i));
        }
        //exercise subSequence() and length();
        int start = random(s.length() - 1);
```

```
    int end = random(s.length() - 1 - start) + start;
    System.out.println(s.subSequence(start, end));
    //exercise toString();
    System.out.println(s);
    }
}
```

6.7 Java Package

1. Java Package
2. Example of package
3. Accessing package
1.   By import packagename.*
2.   By import packagename.classname
3.   By fully qualified name
4. Subpackage
5. Sending class file to another directory
6. -classpath switch
7. 4 ways to load the class file or jar file
8. How to put two public class in a package
9. Static Import
10. Package class

A **java package** is a group of similar types of classes, interfaces and sub-packages.
Package in java can be categorized in two form, built-in package and user-defined package.
There are many built-in packages such as java, lang, awt, javax, swing, net, io, util, sql etc.
Here, we will have the detailed learning of creating and using user-defined packages.
Advantage of Java Package
1) Java package is used to categorize the classes and interfaces so that they can be easily maintained.
2) Java package provides access protection.
3) Java package removes naming collision.

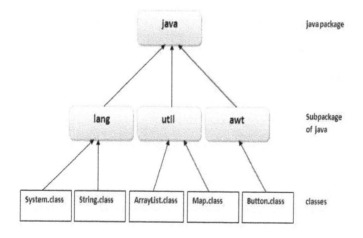

83

Simple example of java package
The **package keyword** is used to create a package in java.
//save as Simple.java
package mypack;
public class Simple
{
public static void main(String args[])
  {
  System.out.println("Welcome to package");
  }
}

How to compile java package
If you are not using any IDE, you need to follow the **syntax** given below:
    javac -d directory javafilename
For **example**
    javac -d . Simple.java
The -d switch specifies the destination where to put the generated class file. You can use any directory name like /home (in case of Linux), d:/abc (in case of windows) etc. If you want to keep the package within the same directory, you can use . (dot).

How to run java package program
You need to use fully qualified name e.g. mypack.Simple etc to run the class.

   To Compile: javac -d . Simple.java

   To Run: java mypack.Simple

Output:Welcome to package

   The -d is a switch that tells the compiler where to put the class file
   i.e. it represents destination. The . represents the current folder.

How to access package from another package?
There are three ways to access the package from outside the package.
    1. import package.*;
    2. import package.classname;
    3. fully qualified name.

1) Using packagename.*
If you use package.* then all the classes and interfaces of this package will be accessible but not subpackages.
The import keyword is used to make the classes and interface of another package accessible to the current package.
Example of package that import the packagename.*
//save by A.java
package pack;
public class A
{
  public void msg(){System.out.println("Hello");}
}

//save by B.java
package mypack;
import pack.*;
class B
{
  public static void main(String args[])

```
{
  A obj = new A();
  obj.msg();
}
}
```
    Output:Hello

2) Using packagename.classname
If you import package.classname then only declared class of this package will be accessible.
Example of package by import package.classname

```
//save by A.java
package pack;
public class A
{
  public void msg(){System.out.println("Hello");}
}
```

```
//save by B.java
package mypack;
import pack.A;
class B
{
  public static void main(String args[]){
   A obj = new A();
   obj.msg();
  }
}
```
    Output:Hello

3) Using fully qualified name
If you use fully qualified name then only declared class of this package will be accessible. Now there is no need to import. But you need to use fully qualified name every time when you are accessing the class or interface.
It is generally used when two packages have same class name e.g. java.util and java.sql packages contain Date class.
Example of package by import fully qualified name

```
//save by A.java
package pack;
public class A
{
  public void msg(){System.out.println("Hello");}
}
```

```
//save by B.java
package mypack;
class B
{
  public static void main(String args[])
{
   pack.A obj = new pack.A();//using fully qualified name
   obj.msg();
}
  }
```

Output:Hello

Note: If you import a package, subpackages will not be imported.
If you import a package, all the classes and interface of that package will be imported excluding the classes and interfaces of the subpackages. Hence, you need to import the subpackage as well.
Note: Sequence of the program must be package then import then class.

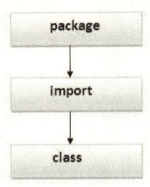

Subpackage in java
Package inside the package is called the **subpackage**. It should be created **to categorize the package further.**
Let's take an example, Sun Microsystem has definded a package named java that contains many classes like System, String, Reader, Writer, Socket etc. These classes represent a particular group e.g. Reader and Writer classes are for Input/Output operation, Socket and ServerSocket classes are for networking etc and so on. So, Sun has subcategorized the java package into subpackages such as lang, net, io etc. and put the Input/Output related classes in io package, Server and ServerSocket classes in net packages and so on.
Example of Subpackage

```
package com.my.core;
class Simple
{
  public static void main(String args[]){
   System.out.println("Hello subpackage");
  }
    }
```

   To Compile: javac -d . Simple.java

   To Run: java com.my.core.Simple

Output:Hello subpackage
How to send the class file to another directory or drive?
There is a scenario, I want to put the class file of A.java source file in classes folder of c: drive. For example:

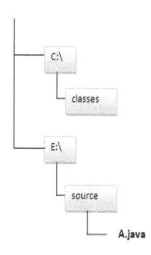

```
//save as Simple.java
package mypack;
public class Simple
{
 public static void main(String args[])
 {
   System.out.println("Welcome to package");
 }
}
```

To Compile:
e:\sources> javac -d c:\classes Simple.java
To Run:

To run this program from e:\source directory, you need to set classpath of the directory where the class file resides.

E:\sources> set classpath=c:\classes;.;

E:\sources> java mypack.Simple

Another way to run this program by -classpath switch of java:
The -classpath switch can be used with javac and java tool.
To run this program from e:\source directory, you can use -classpath switch of java that tells where to look for class file. For example:
e:\sources> java -classpath c:\classes mypack.Simple
Output:Welcome to package

Ways to load the class files or jar files

There are two ways to load the class files temporary and permanent.
- o Temporary
  - o By setting the classpath in the command prompt
  - o By -classpath switch
- o Permanent

- o By setting the classpath in the environment variables
- o By creating the jar file, that contains all the class files, and copying the jar file in the jre/lib/ext folder.

Rule: There can be only one public class in a java source file and it must be saved by the public class name.

//save as C.java otherwise Compilte Time Error
class A{}
class B{}
public class C{}

How to put two public classes in a package?

If you want to put two public classes in a package, have two java source files containing one public class, but keep the package name same. For example:

//save as A.java
package my;
public class A{}

//save as B.java
package javatpoint;
public class B{}

6.8 Access Modifiers in java

1. private access modifier
2. Role of private constructor
3. default access modifier
4. protected access modifier
5. public access modifier
6. Applying access modifier with method overriding

There are two types of modifiers in java: **access modifiers** and **non-access modifiers**.
The access modifiers in java specifies accessibility (scope) of a data member, method, constructor or class.
There are 4 types of java access modifiers:
1. private
2. default
3. protected
4. public

There are many non-access modifiers such as static, abstract, synchronized, native, volatile, transient etc.
Here, we will learn access modifiers.

1) private access modifier
The private access modifier is accessible only within class.

Simple example of private access modifier

In this example, we have created two classes A and Simple. A class contains private data member and private method. We are accessing these private members from outside the class, so there is compile time error.

```
class A
{
private int data=40;
private void msg(){System.out.println("Hello java");}
}

public class Simple
{
 public static void main(String args[])
{
  A obj=new A();
  System.out.println(obj.data);//Compile Time Error
  obj.msg();//Compile Time Error
 }
 }
```

Role of Private Constructor

If you make any class constructor private, you cannot create the instance of that class from outside the class. For example:

```
class A{
private A(){}//private constructor
void msg(){System.out.println("Hello java");}
}
public class Simple{
 public static void main(String args[]){
  A obj=new A();//Compile Time Error
 }
 }
```

Note: A class cannot be private or protected except nested class.

2) default access modifier

If you don't use any modifier, it is treated as **default** bydefault. The default modifier is accessible only within package.

Example of default access modifier

In this example, we have created two packages pack and mypack. We are accessing the A class from outside its package, since A class is not public, so it cannot be accessed from outside the package.

//save by A.java

```
package pack;
class A
{
   void msg(){System.out.println("Hello");}
}
//save by B.java
package mypack;
import pack.*;
class B
{
   public static void main(String args[])
{
   A obj = new A();//Compile Time Error
   obj.msg();//Compile Time Error
}
}
```

In the above example, the scope of class A and its method msg() is default so it cannot be accessed from outside the package.

3) protected access modifier

   The **protected access modifier** is accessible within package and outside the package but through inheritance only.
   The protected access modifier can be applied on the data member, method and constructor. It can't be applied on the class.
   Example of protected access modifier
   In this example, we have created the two packages pack and mypack. The A class of pack package is public, so can be accessed from outside the package. But msg method of this package is declared as protected, so it can be accessed from outside the class only through inheritance.

```
//save by A.java
package pack;
public class A
{
protected void msg(){System.out.println("Hello");}
}
//save by B.java
package mypack;
import pack.*;
class B extends A{
 public static void main(String args[]){
  B obj = new B();
  obj.msg();
 }
}
     Output:Hello
```

4) public access modifier

   The **public access modifier** is accessible everywhere. It has the widest scope among all other modifiers.

Example of public access modifier

```
//save by A.java
package pack;
public class A
{
public void msg(){System.out.println("Hello");}
}
//save by B.java
package mypack;
import pack.*;
class B
{
  public static void main(String args[]){
  A obj = new A();
  obj.msg();
}
}
```

Output:Hello

Understanding all java access modifiers
Let's understand the access modifiers by a simple table.

Access Modifier	Within class	Within package	Outside package by subclass only	Outside package
private	Y	N	N	N
default	Y	Y	N	N
protected	Y	Y	Y	N
public	Y	Y	Y	Y

SUMMARY:

In this chapter you we learn more about interfaces, its syntax and use, the difference between interfaces and abstract class with examples. We also learn the concept of inheritance within interface.

7

EXCEPTION HANDLING

Unit Structure

7.1 OBJECTIVE

In this lesson of Java Tutorial, you will learn...

    The exception handling mechanism.

    Write try ... catch structures to catch expected exceptions.
    Use finally blocks to guarantee execution of code.
    Throw/ Throws exceptions.

7.2 INTRODUCTION

      An exception is an event, which occurs during the execution of the program, that an interrupt the normal flow of the program's instruction. In other words, Exceptions are generated when a recognized condition, usually an error condition, arises during the execution of a method. Java includes a system for running exceptions, by tracking the potential for each method to throw specific exceptions. For each method that could throw an exception, your code must report to the Java compiler that it could throw that exact exception. The compiler marks that method as potentially throwing that exception, and then need any code calling the method to handle the possible exception. Exception handling is basically use five keyword as follows:

- try
- catch
- throw
- throws
- finally

7.3 OVERVIEW

Exceptions are generated when an error condition occur during the execution of a method. It is possible that a statement might throw more than one kind of exception. Exception can be generated by Java-runtime system or they can be manually generated by code. Error-Handling becomes a necessary while developing an application to account for exceptional situations that may occur during the program execution, such as

- Run out of memory
- Resource allocation Error
- Inability to find a file
- Problems in Network connectivity.

In this unit we will learn the exception handling mechanism.

WHAT IS EXCEPTIONS AND HANDLING EXCEPTION?

Exceptions are generated when a recognized an error condition during the execution of a program. Java includes a system for running exceptions, by tracking the potential for each method to throw specific exceptions

- for each method that could throw an exception, your code must report to the Java compiler that it could throw that exact exception.
- the compiler marks that method as potentially throwing that exception, and then need any code calling the method to handle the possible exception.

There are two ways to handle an exception:

- you can try the "risky" code, catch the exception, and do something about it, after which the transmission of the exception come to an end
- you can mark that this method throws that exception, in which case the Java runtime engine will throw the exception back to the method.

So, if you use a method in your code that is marked as throwing a particular exception, the compiler will not allow that code unless you handle the exception. If the exception occurs in a try block, the JVM looks to the catch block(s) that follow to see if any of them equivalent the exception type. The first one that matches will be executed. If none match, then this methods ends, and execution jumps to the method that called this one, at the point the call was made.

Following figure shows the Exception type.

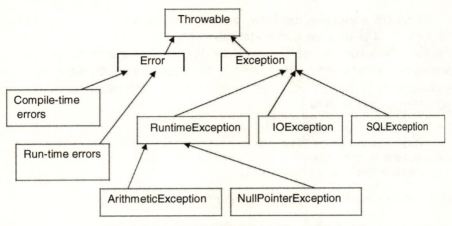

Figure 7.1. A partial view of the Throwable family

An error means fault and there are two types of error as follows:

7.3.1 Compile time errors

Compiler time error means Java compiler identify the syntax error at the time of compilation. And without successfully compilation, compiler does not create .class file. That means we have to compile the program which should be error free and then compiler creates .class file of the program and then we can run the program.
The common problems are:
- Missing braces
- Missing semicolon
- Missing double quote in string
- = instead of == operator
- And so on.

For example: class Try1
{
public static void main(String args[])
{
int a=12; int b=0; int
c=a/b
System.out.println("Division is+c);
}
}
Output:
C:\cc>javac Try1.java Try1.java:8: ';' expected
System.out.println("Division is+c);
^

Try1.java:8: unclosed string literal
System.out.println("Division is+c);
^
2 errors

7.3.2 Run time errors

Several time program may compile successfully and compiler creates the .class file of the program but when the time of running the program, it shows the error and that type of error called run time error.

The common problems are:
- Divide by zero
- Conversion of invalid string to number
- access the element that is out of bound of an array
- Passing the parameters with invalid range.
And so on.
For example:
write a program to find out division of two numbers. class Try1

```
{
public static void main(String args[])
{
int a=12; int b=0; int
c=a/b;
System.out.println("Division is"+c);
}
}
```

Output:
C:\cc>javac Try1.java
C:\cc>java Try1
Exception in thread "main" java.lang.ArithmeticException: / by zero at
Try1.main(Try1.java:7)

7.3.3 try...catch:

If a method is going to resolve potential exception internally, the line of code that could generate the exception is placed inside a try block

there may be other code inside the try block, before and/or after the risky line(s) - any code that depends upon the risky code's success should be in the try block, since it will automatically be skipped if the exception occurs
Syntax –

```
try
{
        code risky/unsafe code
        code that depends on the risky code succeeding
}
```

There is usually at least one catch block immediately after the try block a catch block must specify what type of exception it will catch

Syntax –
```
        catch (ExceptionClassName exceptionObjectName)
        {
                code using methods from exceptionObjectName
        }
```

- there can be more than one catch block, each one marked for a correct exception class
- the exception class that is caught can be any class in the exception hierarchy, either a general (base) class, or a very correct (derived) class
- the catch block(s) must handle all checked exceptions that the try block is known to throw unless you want to throw that exception back to the method.
- it is possible to have a try block without any catch blocks if you have a finally block but any checked exceptions still need to be caught, or the method needs to declare that it throws them

If an exception occurs within a try block, execution jumps to the first catch block whose exception class matches the exception that occurred. Any steps remaining in the try block are skipped. If no exception occurs, then the catch blocks are skipped.

If declare a variable within a try block, it will not exist outside the try block, since the curly braces define the scope of the variable. You will often need that variable later, if nowhere else other than the catch or finally blocks, so you would need to declare the variable before the try.

If you declare but don't initialize a variable before a try block, and the only place you set a value for that variable is in the try block, then it is possible when execution leaves the try ... catch structure that the variable never received a value. So, you would get a "possibly uninitialized value" error message from the compiler, since it actually keeps track of that sort of thing. Usually this happens with object references; you would also generally initialize them to null.

```java
public class demo
        {
        public static void main(String[] args)

        {
                int ans1, ans2;
                int a = 2, b = 2, c = 0;
                try

                {
                        ans1 = a/b;
                        System.out.println("a/b = " + ans1);
                        ans2 = a/c;
                        System.out.println("a/c = " + ans2);

                }
                catch(ArithmeticException e)
```

```
                {
                System.out.println("Arithmetic Exception!");
                }
                System.out.println("demo is over");
        }
}
```

Output:
C:\>set path=C:\Java\jdk1.5.0_01\bin
C:\>javac demo.java
C:\>java demo
a/b = 1
Arithmetic Exception!
demo is over

Code Explanation –
The program will print the first result, and then not succeed while performing the division for the second equation. Execution will step to the catch block to print our message on the screen.

Example -
The prior example used a RuntimeException, which your code is not obligated to handle. Most methods in the I/O classes throw IOException, which is an exception that you must handle.
Following program shows the use of IOException.

```
import java.io.IOException;
public class demo
    {
    public static void main(String[] args)
        {
        int num = 0;
        num = System.in.read();
        try
        {
        num = System.in.read();
        System.out.println("You entered " + (char) num);
        }
        catch (IOException e)
        {
        System.out.println("IO Exception occurred");
        }
        }
    }
```

Output:
C:\>javac demo.java
demo.java:11: unreported exception java.io.IOException; must be caught or declared to be thrown

```
        num = System.in.read(); // comment out this line
             ^
```

1 error

Code Explanation:
The line marked to comment out throws IOException, but is not in a try block, so the compiler rejects it. The second read attempt is within a try block, as it should be. there is no way we can force an IOException from the keyboard to test the catch block.

Using Multiple catch Blocks
It is possible that a statement might throw more than one
kind of exception
- you can list a sequence of catch blocks, one for each possible exception
- remember that there is an object hierarchy for exceptions –

```
class demo
{
public static void main (String args [])
{
int A[ ] = new int [5];

try

{
for (int c = 0; c <5; c++)
{
 //do nothing
}
for (int c = 0; c <5; c++)
{
 A[c] = c/ c;
}
}
    catch (ArrayIndexOutOfBoundsException e)
{
   System.out.println ("Array out of bound ");
}
    catch (ArithmeticException e)
{
   System.out.println ("Zero divide error");
}
}
}
```
Output:
C:\>javac demo.java
C:\>java demo
Zero divide error
C:\>

7.3.5 Finally Block
To guarantee that a line of code runs, whether an exception occurs or not, use a finally block after the try and catch blocks

The code in the finally block will *almost always* execute, even if an unhandled exception occurs; in fact, even if a return statement is encountered

- if an exception causes a catch block to execute, the finally block will be executed after the catch block
- if an uncaught exception occurs, the finally block executes, and then execution exits this method and the exception is thrown to the method that called this method.

Syntax –
```
try
{
risky code/ unsafe code block
}
catch (ExceptionClassName exceptionObjectName)
{
code to resolve problem
}
finally
{
code that will always execute
}
```

In summary:

- a try block is followed by zero or more catch blocks
- There may one finally block as the last block in the structure.
- There must be at least one block from the collective set of catch and finally after the try.

It's possible to have a try block followed by a finally block, with no catch block this is used to prevent an unchecked exception from exiting the method before cleanup code can be executed

Example:
```
public class demo
{
public static void main(String args[])
{
try
{
System.out.println("Try Block before the error.");
System.out.println(1/0);
System.out.println("Try Block after the error.");
}
catch(java.lang.ArithmeticException e)
```

```
{
System.out.println("Catch Block");
System.out.println("A Stack Trace of the Error:");
e.printStackTrace();
//e.getMessage();
System.out.println("The operation is not possible.");
}
finally
{
System.out.println("Finally Block");
}
System.out.println("demo is over");
}
}
```

Output:

```
C:\>javac demo.java
C:\>java demo
Try Block before the error.
Catch Block
A Stack Trace of the Error:
```

java.lang.ArithmeticException: / by zero at demo.main(demo.java:8)

The operation is not possible.

Finally Block

demo is over

7.3.6 Throwing an Exception
You can throw an exception explicitly using the throw statement.
Example:
   You need to throw an exception when a user enters a wrong student ID or password.
   The throws clause is used to list the types of exception that can be thrown in the execution of a method in a program.

7.3.6.1 Using the throw Statement
1. The throw statement causes termination of the normal flow of control of the java code and prevents the execution of the subsequent statements.
2. The throw clause convey the control to the nearest catch block handling the type of exception object throws.
3. If no such catch block exists, the program terminates.

The throw statement accepts a single argument, which is an object of the Exception class.
Syntax –
throw ThrowableObj

You can use the following code to throw the IllegalStateException exception:

```
class demo
{
static void tdemo()
{
try
{
throw new IllegalStateException ();
}
catch (NullPointerException e)
{
System.out.println ("Not Caught by the catch block inside tdemo ().");
}
}
public static void main (String args[ ])
{
try
{
tdemo();
}
catch(IllegalStateException e)
{
System.out.println("Exception Caught in:"+e);
}
}
}
```

Output
C:\>javac demo.java
C:\>java demo
Exception Caught in:java.lang.IllegalStateException
C:\>

7.3.6.2 Using the throws Statement

The throws statement is used by a method to specify the types of exceptions the method throws. If a method is capable of raising an exception that it does not handle, the method must specify that the exception have to be handled by the calling method.

This is done using the throws statement. The throws clause lists the types of exceptions that a method might throw.

Syntax –

[< access specifier >] [< modifier >] < return type > < method name > [< arg list >] [throws <exception list >]

Example:
You can use the following code to use the throws statement:

```
class demo
{
static void throwMethod ( ) throws ClassNotFoundException
{
System.out.println ("In throwMethod ");
throw new ClassNotFoundException ( );
}
public static void main (String args [ ])
{
try
{
throwMethod ( );
}
catch ( ClassNotFoundException e)
{
System.out.println (" throwMethod has thrown an Exception :" +e);
}
}
}
```

Output
```
C:\>javac demo.java
C:\>java demo
In throwMethod
throw Method has thrown an Exception :java.lang.Class Not Found Exception
```

7.3.9 Creating and Using Your Own Exception Classes
You can create your own exception class by extending an existing exception class
Syntax –
[modifiers] New Exception Class Name extends

ExceptionClassName

```
{
 create constructors that usually delegate to super-constructors
}
```

You could then add any fields or methods that you wish, although often that is not required. You must, however, override any constructors you wish to use: Exception ( ), Exception(String message), Exception(String message, Throwable cause), Exception (Throwable cause). Usually you can just call the equivalent super-constructor. If you extend RuntimeException or one of its subclasses, your exception will be treated as a runtime exception.

When a situation arises for which you would like to throw the exception, use the throw keyword with a new object from your exception class, for example:

Syntax –
throw new ExceptionClassName(messageString);

SUMMARY :

In this lesson of the Java tutorial you have learned:
how Java's exception handling mechanism works
how to try and catch exceptions
about the various types of checked and unchecked exceptions
how to write exception classes
how to throw exceptions

8

I/O PACKAGES

Unit Structure

8.1 INTRODUCTION

Stream is an abstract demonstration of input or output device. By using stream, we can write or read data. To bring in information, a program is open a stream on an information source (a file, memory, a socket) and read information sequentially. In this unit, we will learn the concept of stream, I/O package.

8.2 STREAM:

The Java Input/Output (I/O) is a part of **java.io** package. The **java.io** package contains a relatively large number of classes that support input and output operations. The classes in the package are primarily abstract classes and stream-oriented that define methods and subclasses which allow bytes to be read from and written to files or other input and output sources.

For reading the stream:
Open the stream
Read information
Close the stream

For writing in stream:
Open the stream
Write information
Close the stream

There are two types of stream as follows:

o   Byte stream

o   Character stream

Byte Streams:

It supports 8-bit input and output operations. There are two classes of byte stream

o   InputStream

o   OutputStream

8.2.1.1 Input Stream:

The **InputStream** class is used for reading the data such as a byte and array of bytes from an input source. An input source can be a **file**, a **string**, or **memory** that may contain the data. It is an abstract class that defines the programming interface for all input streams that are inherited from it. An input stream is automatically opened when you create it. You can explicitly close a stream with the **close( )** method, or let it be closed implicitly when the object is found as a garbage.

The subclasses inherited from the **InputStream** class can be seen in a hierarchy manner shown below:

Input Stream
ByteArrayInputStream
FileInputStream
ObjectInputStream
FilterInputStream
PipedInputStream
StringBufferInputStream
FilterInputStream

o   BufferedInputStream
o   DataInputStream
o   LineNumberInputStream
o   PushbackInputStream

OutputStream:

The OutputStream class is a sibling to InputStream that is used for writing byte and array of bytes to an output source. Similar to input sources, an output source can be anything such as a file, a string, or memory containing the data. Like an input stream, an output stream is automatically opened when you create it. You can explicitly close an output stream with the **close( )** method, or let it be closed implicitly when the object is garbage collected.

The classes inherited from the **OutputStream** class can be seen in a hierarchy structure shown below:

Output Stream

      ByteArrayOutputStream

      FileOutputStream

      ObjectOutputStream

      FilterInputStream

      PipedOutputStream

      StringBufferInputStream

      FilterOutputStream

              o   BufferedOutputStream

              o   DataOutputStream

              o   PrintStream

OutputStream is also inherited from the Object class. Each class of the OutputStream provided by the java.io package is intended for a different purpose.

8.2.2 Character Streams:

It supports 16-bit Unicode character input and output. There are two classes of character stream as follows:

o   Reader

o   Writer

These classes allow internationalization of Java I/O and also allow text to be stored using international character encoding.

Reader:

      BufferedReader

                          • LineNumberReader

      CharAraayReader

      PipedReader

      StringReader

      FilterReader

                          • PushbackReader

      InputStreamReader

                          • FileReader

Writer:

     BufferedWriter

     CharAraayWriter

     FileWriter

     PipedWriter

     PrintWriter

     String Writer

     OutputStreamWriter

            ■ FileWriter

8.3 HOW FILES AND STREAMS WORK:

Java uses **streams** to handle I/O operations through which the data is flowed from one location to another. For example, an **InputStream** can flow the data from a disk file to the internal memory and an **OutputStream** can flow the data from the internal memory to a disk file. The disk-file may be a text file or a binary file. When we work with a text file, we use a **character** stream where one character is treated as per byte on disk. When we work with a binary file, we use a **binary** stream.

The working process of the I/O streams can be shown in the given diagram.

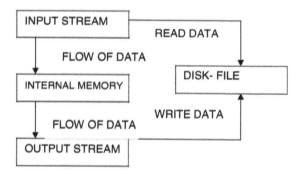

8.4 CLASSES:

The following lists of classes are provided by the **java.io** package shown in the table:

Class	Description
BufferedInputStream	It used for creating an internal buffer array. It supports the mark and reset methods.
Buffered Output Stream	This class used for writes byte to output stream. It implements a bufferedoutput stream.
Buffered Reader	This class provides read text from character input stream and buffering characters. It also reads characters, arrays and lines.
Buffered Writer	This class provides write text from character output stream and buffering characters. It also writes characters, arrays and lines.
ByteArrayInput Stream	It contains the internal buffer and read data from the stream.

ByteArrayOutput Stream	This class used for data is written into byte array. This is implemented in output stream class.
CharArrayReader	It used for char input stream and implements a character buffer.
CharArrayWriter	This class also implements a character buffer and it uses an writer.
DataInput Stream	This class reads the primitive data types from the input stream in a machine format.
DataOutputStream	This class writes the primitive data types from the output stream in machine format.
File	This class shows a file and directory pathnames.
File Descriptor	This class uses for create a FileInputStream and FileOutputStream.
FileInputStream	It contains the input byte from a file and implements an input stream.
FileOutputStream	It uses for writing data to a file and also implements an output stream.
FilePermission	It provides the permission to access a file or directory.
FileReader	This class used for reading characters file.
FileWriter	This class used for writing characters files.
InputStream	This class represents an input stream of bytes.
InputStreamReader	It reads bytes and decodes them into characters.
LineNumberReader	This class has a line numbers
ObjectInputStream	This class used for recover the object to serialize previously.
ObjectInputStream. GetField	This class access to president fields read from input stream.

8.5 EXCEPTIONS CLASSES:

The following summary of the exception classes provided by the **java.io** package shown in the table:

Exceptions	Description
Char Conversion Exception	It provides detail message in the catch block to associated with the CharConversionException
EOF Exception	This exception indicates the end of file. When the file input stream is to be end then the EOFException is to be occured.
FileNotFound Exception	When the opened file's pathname does not find then this exception occurs.
InterruptedIO Exception	When the I/O operations are interrupted from any causes then it occurs.
InvalidClassException	Any problems to be created with class, when the Serializing runtime to be detected.
InvalidObject Exception	When the de-serialized objects fails then it occurs.
IOException	When the I/O operations fail then it occurs.
NotActive Exception	The Serialization or deserialization operations are not active then it occurs.
NotSerializable Exception	This exception occurs when the instance is required to be a Serializable interface.
ObjectStream Exception	This is a supper class of all exception class. It is used for specific Object Stream Classes.
WriteAborted Exception	In this exception to be thrown by the ObjectStreamException during a write operating.

8.6 STANDARD STREAMS

Standard Streams are a feature provided by many operating systems. By default, they read input from the keyboard and write output to the display. They also support I/O operations on files.

Standard Input: - Accessed through **System.in** which is used to read input from the keyboard.

Standard Output: - Accessed through **System.out** which is used to write output to be display.

Standard Error: - Accessed through **System.err** which is used to write error output to be display.

Java also supports three Standard Streams:
These objects are defined automatically and do not need to be opened explicitly.

Standard Output and Standard Error, both are to write output; having error output separately so that the user may read error messages efficiently.

System.in is a byte stream that has no character stream features. To use Standard Input as a character stream, wrap System.in within the InputStreamReader as an argument.

InputStreamReader inp= new InputStreamReader (System.in);

8.7 WORKING WITH READER CLASSES

Java provides the standard I/O facilities for reading text from either the file or the keyboard on the command line. The **Reader** class is used for this purpose that is available in the **java.io** package. It acts as an abstract class for reading character streams. The only methods that a subclass must implement are **read(char[], int, int)** and **close()**. The Reader class is further categorized into the subclasses.

The following diagram shows a class-hierarchy of the **java.io.Reader** class.

However, most subclasses override some of the methods in order to provide higher efficiency, additional functionality, or both.

8.7.1 InputStreamReader:

An InputStreamReader is a bridge from byte streams to character streams i.e. it reads bytes and decodes them into Unicode characters according to a particular platform. Thus, this class reads characters from a byte input stream. When you create an InputStreamReader, you specify an InputStream from which, the InputStreamReader reads the bytes.

The syntax of InputStreamReader is written as:

InputStreamReader<variable_name>= new InputStreamReader (System.in)

8.7.2 BufferedReader:

The BufferedReader class is the subclass of the Reader class. It reads character-input stream data from a memory area known as a buffer maintains state. The buffer size may be specified, or the default size may be used that is large enough for text reading purposes.

BufferedReader converts an unbuffered stream into a buffered stream using the wrapping expression, where the unbuffered stream object is passed to the constructor for a buffered stream class.

For example the constructors of the BufferedReader class shown as:

BufferedReader (Reader in): Creates a buffering character-input stream that uses a default-sized input buffer.

BufferedReader (Reader in, int sz): Creates a buffering character-input stream that uses an input buffer of the specified size.

BufferedReader class provides some standard methods to perform specific reading operations shown in the table. All methods throw an IOException, if an I/O error occurs.

Method	Return Type	Description
read( )	int	Reads a single character
read(char[ ] cbuf, int off, int len)	int	Read characters into a portion of an array.
readLine( )	String	Read a line of text. A line is considered to be terminated by ('\n').
close( )	void	Closes the opened stream.

This program illustrates use of standard input stream to read the user input.

```
import java.io.*;
public class ReadStandardIO
{
  public static void main(String[] args) throws IOException
   {
     InputStreamReader inp = new InputStreamReader(System.in)
     BufferedReader br = new BufferedReader(inp);
     System.out.println("Enter text : ");
    String str = in.readLine();
     System.out.println("You entered String : ");
     System.out.println(str);
 }
}
```

Output of the Program:
C:\>javac ReadStandardIO.java C:\>java

ReadStandardIO Enter text:

this is an Input Stream You entered

String: this is an Input Stream C:\>

The streams provide a simple model for reading and writing data. However, streams don't support all the operations that are common with a disk file. Now, we will learn how to work with a file using the non-stream file I/O.

The File class deals with the machine dependent files in a machine-independent manner i.e. it is easier to write platform-independent code that examines and manipulates files using the File class. This class is available in the java.lang package.

The java.io.File is the central class that works with files and directories. The instance of this class represents the name of a file or directory on the host file system.

When a File object is created, the system doesn't check to the existence of a corresponding file/directory. If the files exist, a program can examine its attributes and perform various operations on the file, such as renaming it, deleting it, reading from or writing to it.

The constructors of the File class are shown in the table:

Constructor	Description
File(path)	Create File object for default directory (usually where program is located).
File(dirpath,fname)	Create File object for directory path given as string.
File(dir, fname)	Create File object for directory.

Thus the statement can be written as:
File f = new File ("<filename>");

The methods that are used with the file object to get the attribute of a corresponding file shown in the table.

Method	Description
f.exists()	Returns true if file exists.
f.isFile()	Returns true if this is a normal file.
f.isDirectory()	true if "f" is a directory.
f.getName()	Returns name of the file or directory.
f.isHidden()	Returns true if file is hidden.
f.lastModified()	Returns time of last modification.
f.length()	Returns number of bytes in file.
f.getPath()	Path name.
f.delete()	Deletes the file.
f.renameTo(f2)	Renames f to File f2. Returns true if successful.
f.createNewFile()	Creates a file and may throw IOException.

Whenever the data is needed to be stored, a file is used to store the data. File is a collection of stored information that is arranged in string, rows, columns and lines etc. Further, we will see how to create a file. This example takes the file name and text data for storing to the file.

For creating a new file File.createNewFile ( ) method is used. This method returns a boolean value true if the file is created otherwise return false. If the mentioned file for the specified directory is already exist then the createNewFile () method returns the false otherwise the method creates the mentioned file and return true.

Let's see an example that checks the existence of a specified file.

```
import java.io.*;
public class CreateFile1
{
    public static void main(String[] args) throws IOException

        {
        File f;
        f=new File ("myfile.txt"); if(!f.exists()){
        f.createNewFile();
        System.out.println("New file \"myfile.txt\" has been created to the current
                directory");
        }
    }
}
```

First, this program checks, the specified file **"myfile.txt"** is exist or not. If it does not exist then a new file is created with same name to the current location.

Output of the Program

C:\>javac CreateFile1.java
C:\>java CreateFile1
New file "myfile.txt" has been created to the current directory
C:\>

If you try to run this program again then after checking the existence of the file, it will not be created and you will see a message as shown in the output.

C:\>javac CreateFile1.java
C:\>java CreateFile1
the specified file is already exist
C:\>

In Java, it is possible to set dynamic path, which is helpful for mapping local file name with the actual path of the file using the constructing filename path technique.

As seen, how a file is created to the current directory where the program is run. Now we will see how the same program constructs a File object from a more complicated file name, using the static constant File.separator or File.separatorCharto specify the file name in a platform-independent way. If we are using Windows platform then the value of this separator is ' \ '.

Let's see an example to create a file to the specified location.

```
import java.io.*;
public class PathFile
{
    public static void main(String[] args) throws IOException
    {
        File f;
```

```
                f=new File ("example" + File.separator + "myfile.txt");
                f.createNewFile ();
                System.out.println("New file \"myfile.txt\" has been created
                        to the specified location");
                System.out.println ("The absolute path of the file is: "
                                +f.getAbsolutePath ());
}
}
```

Output of the program:
C:\>javac PathFile.java
C:\>java PathFile
New file "myfile.txt" has been created to the specified location the absolute

path of the file is: C:\Shubh\example\myfile.txt

C:\>

8.8 I/O STREAMS:

Let's now see some I/O streams that are used to perform reading and writing operation in a file. Java supports the following I/O file streams.

FileInputstream

FileOutputStream

8.8.1 FileInputstream:

This class is a subclass of Inputstream class that reads bytes from a specified file name. The read () method of this class reads a byte or array of bytes from the file. It returns -1 when the end-of-file has been reached. We typically use this class in conjunction with a BufferedInputStream and DataInputstream class to read binary data. To read text data, this class is used with an InputStreamReader and BufferedReader class. This class throws FileNotFoundException, if the specified file is not exist. You can use the constructor of this stream as:

FileInputstream (File filename);

8.8.2 FileOutputStream:-

This class is a subclass of OutputStream that writes data to a specified file name. The write () method of this class writes a byte or array of bytes to the file. We typically use this class in conjunction with a BufferedOutputStream and a DataOutputStream class to write binary data. To write text, we typically use it with a PrintWriter, BufferedWriter and an OutputStreamWriter class. You can use the constructor of this stream as:

FileOutputstream (File filename);

8.8.3 DataInputStream:-

This class is a type of FilterInputStream that allows you to read binary data of Java primitive data types in a portable way. In other words, the DataInputStream class is used to read binary Java primitive data types in a machine-independent way.

An application uses a DataOutputStream to write data that can later be read by a DataInputStream. You can use the constructor of this stream as:

DataInputStream (FileOutputstream finp);

The following program demonstrates how contains are read from a file.

```java
import java.io.*;
public class ReadFile
{
    public static void main(String[] args) throws IOException
{
    File f;
    f=new File("myfile.txt");
    if(!f.exists()&& f.length()<0)
    System.out.println("The specified file is not exist");
    else
    {
      FileInputStream finp=new FileInputStream(f); byte b;
      do{
      b=(byte)finp.read();
      System.out.print((char)b);
        }while(b!=-1); finp.close();
    }

}
}
```

Output of the Program:

C:\>javac ReadFile.java
C:\>java ReadFile this is a text
file? C:\>

This program reads the bytes from file and displays it to the user.

Now we will learn how to write data to a file. As discussed, the FileOutputStream class is used to write data to a file.

Let's see an example that writes the data to a file converting into the bytes.

This program first checks the existence of the specified file. If the file exists, the data is written to the file through the object of the FileOutputStream class.

```java
import java.io.*;
public class WriteFile
{
    public static void main(String[] args) throws IOException
    {
    File f=new File ("textfile1.txt");
    FileOutputStream fop=new FileOutputStream (f);
    if (f.exists ())
    {
    String str="This data is written through the program";
```

```
        fop.write (str.getBytes ());
        fop.flush (); fop.close ();
        System.out.println ("The data has been written");
        }
        else
          System.out.println ("This file is not exist");
    }
}
```

Output of the Program
C:\>javac WriteFile.java
C:\>java WriteFile

The data has been written
C:\>

Now, you will learn how to count the availability of text lines in the particular file. A file is read before counting lines of a particular file. File is a collection of stored information that is arranged in string, rows, columns and lines etc. Try it for getting the lines through the following program

Description of program:

The following program helps you in counting lines of a particular file. At the execution time of this program, it takes a file name with its extension from a particular directory and checks it using exists () method. If the file exists, it will count lines of a particular file otherwise it will display a message **"File does not exists!"**

Description of code:
FileReader (File file):

This is the constructor of **FileReader** class that is reliable for reading a character files. It constructs a new **FileReader** and takes a file name that have to be read.

FileNumberReader ():

This is the constructor of **FileNumberReader** class. It constructs a new line-numbering reader. It reads characters and puts into buffer. By default the numbering of line begins from '**0**'.

Here is the code of program:
```
import java.io.*;
public class NumberOfLine{
public static void main(String[] args) {
  try{
    System.out.println("Getting line number of a particular file exam ple!");
    BufferedReader bf = new BufferedReader(new InputStreamRea der(System.in));
    System.out.println("Please enter file name with extension:");
    String str = bf.readLine();
    File file = new File(str);
    if (file.exists()){
    FileReader fr = new FileReader(file);
    LineNumberReader In = new LineNumberReader(fr);
    int count = 0;
    while (In.readLine() != null){
```

```
        count++;
    }
     System.out.println("Total line no: " + count);
      ln.close();
     }
     else{
      System.out.println("File does not exists!");
     }

   }catch(IOException e){
     e.printStackTrace();
    }
  }
}
```

Output of program:
Getting line number of a particular file example!
Please enter file name with extension:
AddTwoBigNumbers.shtml
Total line no: 58

Java provides the facility for changing a file timestamp according to the user reliability.

Description of program:

This program helps you in changing a file timestamp or modification time in Java. After running this program it will take a file name and its modification date in **'dd-mm-yyyy'** format. Then it will check the given file is exist or not using **exists ()** method. When the file exists, this program will change the date of given file and it will display a message **"Modification is successfully!"** otherwise it will show **"File does not exists!"**

Description of code:

setLastModified(long time):

This is the method that sets the last modification time of a file or directory and returns Boolean types values either **'true'** or **'false'**. If it will return a 'true' only when the modification is completely successfully otherwise, it will return 'false'. This method takes following long type data:

time:
This is the time that has to be modified or set.

getTime ():
This is the method that returns the number of milliseconds in GMT format like: 23-04-2007.

Here is the code of program:
import java.io.*; import java.util.*;

import java.text.*;
public class ChangeFileDate{
public static void main(String[] args) { try{

118

```
System.out.println("Change file timestamp example!");
BufferedReader bf = new BufferedReader(new InputStreamRea der(System.in));
System.out.println("Enter file name with extension:");

String str = bf.readLine();

System.out.println("Enter last modified date in 'dd-mm-yyyy' format:");
String strDate = bf.readLine();
SimpleDateFormat sdf= new SimpleDateFormat("dd-MM-yyyy");

Date date = sdf.parse(strDate);

File file = new File(str); if (file.exists()){

    file.setLastModified(date.getTime());

    System.out.println("Modification is successfully!");

}
  else{
    System.out.println("File does not exists!");
  }
}catch(Exception e){
  e.printStackTrace();
  }
}
```

Output of program:
Change file timestamp example! Enter file name
with extension: StrStartWith.shtml
Enter last modified date in 'dd-mm-yyyy' format: 23-04-2007
Modification is successfully

8.9 FINDING A FILE

To find a file or directory it is very necessary to know the path of the file or directory so that you can access it. If you know the path then it is very easy to work on it. Suppose a situation where a problem comes in front you where you don't know the path of the file, then what will you do? This problem can be solved by using a method getAbsolutePath ().The method getAbsolutePath () should be used where we don't know the exact path of the file.

To find an absolute path of a file, Firstly we have to make a class **GetAbsolutePath**. Inside this class, define the main method. Inside this method define a File class of java.io package. Inside the constructor of a File class pass the name of the file whose absolute path you want to know. Now call the method *getAbsolutePath ()* of the **File** class by the reference of File class and store it in a String variable. Now print the string, you will get an absolute path of the file.

In this class we have make use of the following things by which this problem can be solved.

File: It is class in java.io package. It implements Comparable and Serializable interface.

getAbsolutePath (): It returns the absolute path name in the form of string.

Code of the program is given below:
```
import java.io.*;
public class  GetAbsolutePath
{
 public static void main(String[ ] args)

{
String str = args[0];
File file = new File(str);
String absolutePathOfFirstFile = file.getAbsolutePath();
System.out.println(" The absolute path in first form is "
                                    + absolutePathOfFirstFile);
 file = new File( "Happy" + File.separatorChar+ str);
 String absolutePathOfSecondFile = file.getAbsolutePath();
System.out.println(" The absolute path is " + absolutePathOfSecondFile);
file = new File("Happy" + File.separator + ".." + File.separator + str);
String absolutePathOfThirdFile = file.getAbsolutePath ();
System.out.println(" The absolute path is" + absolutePathOfThirdFile);
}
```

Output of the program
Happy
The absolute path in first form is C:\Smile\Happy
The absolute path is C:\Smile\Happy\Happy
The absolute path is C:\Smile\Happy\..\Happy

8.10 SUMMARY:

In this unit, we learn that what is stream and types of stream. We also learn the concept of input and output stream (The Java Input/Output (I/O) is a part of **java.io** package). The **java.io** package contains a relatively large number of classes that support input and output operations.

9

MULTI THREADING

Unit Structure
Objective: In this lesson of Java Tutorial, you will learn...
Introduction:
Overview:
Thread Life cycle:
>Advantages of multithreading over multi-tasking:
>Thread Creation and simple programs:
>Synchronized threads:
>>Synchronized Methods:

9.1 OBJECTIVE:

In this lesson of Java Tutorial, you will learn...

Thread life cycle
How to create thread
Advantages of threading

9.2 INTRODUCTION

A *thread* is defined as a separate stream of implementation that takes place simultaneously with and independently of everything else that might be happening. It does not have an event loop. A thread runs autonomously of anything else happening in the computer. With threads the other tasks that don't get stuck in the loop can continue processing without waiting for the stuck task to terminate. A thread is a coding that doesn't affect the architecture of an application. Threading is equally separate the computer's power among different tasks.

9.3 OVERVIEW:

Threading concept is very important in Java Programing language. A thread is a sequential path of code execution within a program. And each thread has its own local variables, program counter and lifetime.

In Java, an object of the Thread class can represent a thread. Thread can be implemented through any one of two ways:

Using threads in Java will enable greater flexibility to programmers looking for that extra edge in their programs. The simplicity of creating, configuring and running threads lets Java programmers devise portable and powerful applets/applications that cannot be made in other third-generation languages. Threads allow any program to perform multiple tasks at once. In an Internet-aware language such as Java, this is a very important tool.

9.4 THREAD LIFE CYCLE:

When you are programming with threads, understanding the life cycle of thread is very valuable. While a thread is alive, it is in one of several states. By invoking start () method, it doesn't mean that the thread has access to CPU and start executing straight away. Several factors determine how it will proceed.

Different states of a thread are:

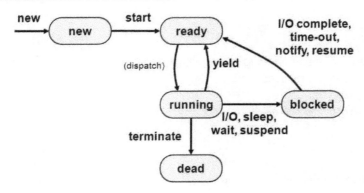

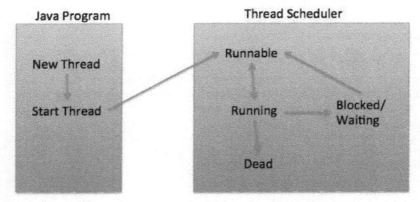

1. New state – After the construction of Thread instance the thread is in this state but before the start() method invocation. At this point, the thread is considered not alive.

2. Runnable (Ready-to-run) state – A thread start its life from Runnable state. A thread first enters runnable state after the
invoking of start() method but a thread can come again to this state after either running, waiting, sleeping or coming back from blocked state also. On this state a thread is waiting for a turn on the processor.

3. Running state – A thread is in running state that means the thread is presently executing. There are numerous ways to enter in Runnable state but there is only one way to enter in Running state: the scheduler select a thread from runnable pool.

4. Dead state – A thread can be considered dead when its run() method completes. If any thread comes on this state that means it cannot ever run again.

5. Blocked - A thread can enter in this state because of waiting the resources that are hold by another thread.

Advantages of multithreading over multi-tasking:
1. Reduces the computation time.
2. Improves performance of an application.
3. Threads distribute the same address space so it saves the memory.
4. Context switching between threads is usually less costly than between processes.
5. Cost of communication between threads is comparatively low.

9.4.2 Thread Creation and simple programs:
In Java, an object of the Thread class can represent a thread. Thread can be implemented through any one of two ways:

1. Extending the java.lang.Thread Class

2. Implementing the java.lang.Runnable Interface

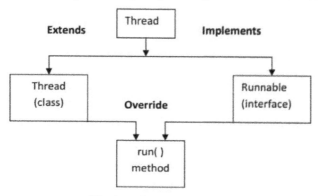

Fig 9.3: Creation of thread

Extending the java.lang.Thread Class
Syntax:
```
class MyThread extends Thread
    {
    }
```

Implementing the java.lang.Runnable Interface
Syntax:
```
MyThread implements Runnable
    {
    }
```

123

1. After declaration of thread class, we have to override run( ) method in class.

2. Now we can create object of thread if needed.

In short we have to follow following these steps:
1. Extend the java.lang.Thread Class.
2. Override the run( ) method in the subclass from the Thread class to define the code executed by the thread.
3. Create an instance of this subclass. This subclass may call a Thread class constructor by subclass constructor.
4. Invoke the start( ) method on the instance of the class to make the thread eligible for running.

The following program demonstrates a single thread creation extending the "Thread" Class:

```
class MyThread extends Thread
{
String s=null; MyThread(String s1)
        {
                s=s1;
                start();
        }
        public void run()
        {
                System.out.println(s);
        }
}

public class RunThread

{
        public static void main(String args[])

        {
                MyThread m1=new MyThread("Thread started....");
        }
}
```

Output of the Program is:
C:\>javac RunThread.java
C:\>java RunThread
Thread started....
II. Implementing the java.lang.Runnable Interface
The procedure for creating threads by implementing the Runnable Interface is as follows:
1. A Class implements the Runnable Interface, override the run() method to define the code executed by thread. An object of this class is Runnable Object.
2. Create an object of Thread Class by passing a Runnable object as argument.
3. Invoke the start( ) method on the instance of the Thread class.

The following program demonstrates the thread creation implenting the Runnable interface:

```
class Thr1 implements Runnable
{
Thread t;
  String s=null;
    Thr1(String s1){ s=s1;
    t=new Thread(this); t.start();
}

public void run()
{
System.out.println(s);
}

}

public class RunableThread
{
  public static void main(String args[])
  {
  Thr1 m1=new Thr1("Thread started....");
  }
}
```

Output:
C:\>javac RunableThread.java
C:\>java RunableThread
Thread started....

However, this program returns the output same as of the output generated through the previous program.There are two reasons for implementing a Runnable interface preferable to extending the Thread Class:

1. If you extend the Thread Class, that means that subclass cannot extend any other Class, but if you implement Runnable interface then you can do this.

2. The class implementing the Runnable interface can avoid the full overhead of Thread class which can be excessive.

join() & isAlive() methods:
The following program demonstrates the join() & isAlive() methods:

```
class DemoAlive extends Thread { int value;
  public DemoAlive(String str)
  {
    super(str);
    value=0;
    start();
  }

public void run()
      {
      try
```

```
        {
        while (value < 5) {
        System.out.println(getName() + ": " + (value++));
            Thread.sleep(250);
        }
    } catch (Exception e) {}
    System.out.println("Exit from thread: " + getName());
    }
}

public class DemoJoin
{
    public static void main(String[] args)
        {
        DemoAlive da = new DemoAlive("Thread a");
        DemoAlive db = new DemoAlive("Thread b");
        try
            {
            System.out.println("Wait for the child threads to finish."); da.join();
            if (!da.isAlive())
                System.out.println("Thread A not alive."); db.join();
            if (!db.isAlive())
                System.out.println("Thread B not alive.");
            } catch (Exception e) { } System.out.println("Exit from Main Thread.");
    }
}
```

Output:
```
C:\>javac DemoJoin.java
C:\>java DemoJoin
Wait for the child threads to finish.
Thread a: 0
Thread b: 0
Thread a: 1
Thread b: 1
Thread a: 2
Thread b: 2
Thread a: 3
Thread b: 3
Thread a: 4
Thread b: 4
Exit from thread: Thread a
Thread A not alive.
Exit from thread: Thread b
Thread B not alive.
Exit from Main Thread.
```

9.4.3 Synchronized threads:

In Java, the threads are executed separately to each other. These types of threads are called as asynchronous threads. But there are two problems may be occurs with asynchronous threads.

126

1. Two or more threads share the similar resource (variable or method) while only one of them can access the resource at one time.

2. If the producer and the consumer are sharing the same kind of data in a program then either producer may make the data faster or consumer may retrieve an order of data and process it without its existing.

Suppose, we have created two methods as increment( ) and decrement( ). which increases or decreases value of the variable "count" by 1 respectively shown as:

public void increment( ) { count++; }

When the two threads are executed to access these methods (one for increment( ),another for decrement( )) then both will distribute the variable "count". in that case, we can't be sure that what value will be returned of variable "count".

We can see this problem in the diagram shown below:

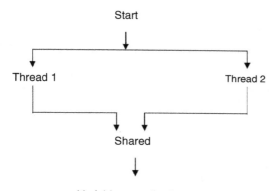

To avoid this problem, Java uses monitor also known as "semaphore" to prevent data from being corrupted by multiple threads by a keyword synchronized to coordinate them and intercommunicate to each other. It is basically a mechanism which allows two or more threads to share all the available resources in a sequential manner. Java's synchronized is used to ensure that only one thread is in a critical region. Critical region is a lock area where only one thread is run (or lock) at a time. Once the thread is in its critical section, no other thread can enter to that critical region. In that case, another thread will has to wait until the current thread leaves its critical section.

General form of the synchronized statement is as:

```
synchronized(object)
{
// statements to be synchronized
}
```

Lock:

Lock term refers to the access approved to a particular thread that can access the shared resources. At any given time, only one thread can hold the lock and thereby have access to the shared resource. Every object in Java has build-in lock that only comes in action when the object has synchronized method code. By associating a shared resource with a Java object and its lock, the object can act as a guard, ensuring synchronized access to the resource. Only one thread at a time can access the shared resource guarded by the object lock.

Since there is one lock per object, if one thread has acquired the lock, no other thread can acquire the lock until the lock is not released by first thread. Acquire the lock means the thread currently in synchronized method and released the lock means exits the synchronized method.

Remember the following points related to lock and synchronization:

1. Only methods (or blocks) can be synchronized, Classes and variable cannot be synchronized.
2. Each object has just one lock.
3. All methods in a class need not to be coordinated. A class can have both synchronized and non-synchronized methods.
4. If two threads wants to execute a synchronized method in a class, and both threads are using the similar instance of the class to invoke the method then only one thread can execute the method at a time.
5. If a class has both synchronized and non-synchronized methods, multiple threads can still access the class's non-synchronized methods. If you have methods that don't access the data you're trying to protect, then you don't need to synchronize them. Synchronization can cause a hit in several cases (or even deadlock if used incorrectly), so you should be careful not to overuse it.
6. If a thread goes to sleep, it holds any locks it has—it doesn't let go them.
7. A thread can obtain more than one lock. For example, a thread can enter a synchronized method, thus acquiring a lock, and then directly invoke a synchronized method on a different object, thus acquiring that lock as well. As the stack unwinds, locks are unrestricted again.
8. You can synchronize a block of code rather than a method.
9. Constructors cannot be synchronized

9.4.3.1 Synchronized Methods:

Any method is specified with the keyword synchronized is only executed by one thread at a time. If any thread wants to implement the synchronized method, firstly it has to obtain the objects lock. If the lock is already held by another thread, then calling thread has to wait.

Synchronized methods are useful in those situations where methods are executed concurrently, so that these can be intercommunicate control the state of an object in ways that can corrupt the state if. Stack implementations usually define the two operations push and pop of elements as synchronized, that's why pushing and popping are mutually exclusive process. For Example - if several threads were sharing a stack, if one thread is popping the element on the stack then another thread would not be able to pushing the element on the stack.

The following program demonstrates the synchronized method:

```
class Demo extends Thread
{
  static String msg[]={"This", "is", "a", "synchronized", "variable"};
  Share(String threadname)
  {
    super(threadname);
  }
  public void run()
  {
  display(getName());
  }
  public synchronized void display(String threadN)
  {
  for(int i=0;i<=4;i++)
     System.out.println(threadN+msg[i]);
     try{
         this.sleep(1000);
         }catch(Exception e){}
   }
}
public class SynThread1
{
  public static void main(String[] args)
  {
    Share t1=new Share("Thread One: "); t1.start();
    Share t2=new Share("Thread Two: "); t2.start();
  }
}
```

Output of the program is:
Thread One: variable
Thread Two: This
Thread Two: is
Thread two: a
Thread Two: synchronized
Thread Two: variable
C:\nisha>javac SynThread.java
C:\nisha>java SynThread
Thread One: This
Thread One: is
Thread One: a
Thread One: synchronized
Thread One: variable
Thread Two: This
Thread Two: is
Thread two: a
Thread Two: synchronized
Thread Two: variable

Thread Concurrency

ThreadLocal Class
The ThreadLocal class is used to create thread local variables which can only be read and written by the same thread. For example, if two threads are accessing code having reference to same threadLocal variable then each thread will not see any modification to threadLocal variable done by other thread.

ThreadLocal Methods
Following is the list of important methods available in the ThreadLocal class.

Sr.No.	Method & Description
1	**public T get()** Returns the value in the current thread's copy of this thread-local variable.
2	**protected T initialValue()** Returns the current thread's "initial value" for this thread-local variable.
3	**public void remove()** Removes the current thread's value for this thread-local variable.
4	**public void set(T value)** Sets the current thread's copy of this thread-local variable to the specified value.

Sets the current thread's copy of this thread-local variable to the specified value.
Example
The following TestThread program demonstrates some of these methods of the ThreadLocal class. Here we've used two counter variable, one is normal variable and another one is ThreadLocal.

```
class RunnableDemo implements Runnable
{
   int counter;
   ThreadLocal<Integer> threadLocalCounter = new ThreadLocal<Integer>();
   public void run()
   {
      counter++;
      if(threadLocalCounter.get() != null)
      {
         threadLocalCounter.set(threadLocalCounter.get().intValue() + 1);
      }
      else
      {
         threadLocalCounter.set(0);
      }
      System.out.println("Counter: " + counter);
      System.out.println("threadLocalCounter: " + threadLocalCounter.get());
   }
}
```

```java
public class TestThread
{
  public static void main(String args[])
  {
    RunnableDemo commonInstance = new RunnableDemo();
    Thread t1 = new Thread(commonInstance);
    Thread t2 = new Thread(commonInstance);
    Thread t3 = new Thread(commonInstance);
    Thread t4 = new Thread(commonInstance);
    t1.start();
    t2.start();
    t3.start();
    t4.start();
    // wait for threads to end
    try {
      t1.join();
      t2.join();
      t3.join();
      t4.join();
    } catch (Exception e) {
      System.out.println("Interrupted");
    }
  }
}
```

This will produce the following result.

Output
Counter: 1
threadLocalCounter: 0
Counter: 2
threadLocalCounter: 0
Counter: 3
threadLocalCounter: 0
Counter: 4
threadLocalCounter: 0

You can see the value of counter is increased by each thread, but threadLocalCounter remains 0 for each thread.

Java Concurrency - Lock Interface

A java.util.concurrent.locks.Lock interface is used to as a thread synchronization mechanism similar to synchronized blocks. New Locking mechanism is more flexible and provides more options than a synchronized block. Main differences between a Lock and a synchronized block are following –

- **Guarantee of sequence** – Synchronized block does not provide any guarantee of sequence in which waiting thread will be given access. Lock interface handles it.

- **No timeout** – Synchronized block has no option of timeout if lock is not granted. Lock interface provides such option.

- **Single method** – Synchronized block must be fully contained within a single method whereas a lock interface's methods lock() and unlock() can be called in different methods.

Lock Methods

Following is the list of important methods available in the Lock class.

Sr.No.	Method & Description
1	**public void lock()** Acquires the lock.
2	**public void lockInterruptibly()** Acquires the lock unless the current thread is interrupted.
3	**public Condition newCondition()** Returns a new Condition instance that is bound to this Lock instance.
4	**public boolean tryLock()** Acquires the lock only if it is free at the time of invocation.
5	**public boolean tryLock()** Acquires the lock only if it is free at the time of invocation.
6	**public boolean tryLock(long time, TimeUnit unit)** Acquires the lock if it is free within the given waiting time and the current thread has not been interrupted.
7	**public void unlock()** Releases the lock.

Example

The following TestThread program demonstrates some of these methods of the Lock interface. Here we've used lock() to acquire the lock and unlock() to release the lock.

```java
import java.util.concurrent.locks.Lock;
import java.util.concurrent.locks.ReentrantLock;
class PrintDemo
{
   private final Lock queueLock = new ReentrantLock();
   public void print() {
     queueLock.lock();
     try {
       Long duration = (long) (Math.random() * 10000);
       System.out.println(Thread.currentThread().getName()
         + " Time Taken " + (duration / 1000) + " seconds.");
       Thread.sleep(duration);
     } catch (InterruptedException e) {
       e.printStackTrace();
     } finally {
       System.out.printf(
         "%s printed the document successfully.\n",
Thread.currentThread().getName());
       queueLock.unlock();
     }
   }
}

class ThreadDemo extends Thread
{
   PrintDemo  printDemo;
   ThreadDemo(String name,  PrintDemo printDemo) {
     super(name);
     this.printDemo = printDemo;
   }
   @Override
   public void run()
{
     System.out.printf(
       "%s starts printing a document\n", Thread.currentThread().getName());
     printDemo.print();
   }
}
```

```java
public class TestThread
{
  public static void main(String args[])
  {
    PrintDemo PD = new PrintDemo();
    ThreadDemo t1 = new ThreadDemo("Thread - 1 ", PD);
    ThreadDemo t2 = new ThreadDemo("Thread - 2 ", PD);
    ThreadDemo t3 = new ThreadDemo("Thread - 3 ", PD);
    ThreadDemo t4 = new ThreadDemo("Thread - 4 ", PD);
    t1.start();
    t2.start();
    t3.start();
    t4.start();
  }
}
```

This will produce the following result.

Output

Thread - 1 starts printing a document
Thread - 4 starts printing a document
Thread - 3 starts printing a document
Thread - 2 starts printing a document
Thread - 1   Time Taken 4 seconds.
Thread - 1 printed the document successfully.
Thread - 4   Time Taken 3 seconds.
Thread - 4 printed the document successfully.
Thread - 3   Time Taken 5 seconds.
Thread - 3 printed the document successfully.
Thread - 2   Time Taken 4 seconds.
Thread - 2 printed the document successfully.

We've use ReentrantLock class as an implementation of Lock interface here. ReentrantLock class allows a thread to lock a method even if it already have the lock on other method.

Java Concurrency - ReadWriteLock Interface

A java.util.concurrent.locks.ReadWriteLock interface allows multiple threads to read at a time but only one thread can write at a time.

- **Read Lock** – If no thread has locked the ReadWriteLock for writing then multiple thread can access the read lock.

- **Write Lock** – If no thread is reading or writing, then one thread can access the write lock.

Lock Methods

Following is the list of important methods available in the Lock class.

Sr.No.	Method & Description
1	**public Lock readLock()** Returns the lock used for reading.
2	**public Lock writeLock()** Returns the lock used for writing.

Example

The following TestThread program demonstrates these methods of the ReadWriteLock interface. Here we've used readlock() to acquire the read-lock and writeLock() to acquire the write-lock.

```
import java.util.concurrent.locks.ReentrantReadWriteLock;
public class TestThread
{
   private static final ReentrantReadWriteLock lock = new
ReentrantReadWriteLock(true);
   private static String message = "a";
   public static void main(String[] args) throws InterruptedException {
      Thread t1 = new Thread(new WriterA());
      t1.setName("Writer A");
      Thread t2 = new Thread(new WriterB());
      t2.setName("Writer B");
      Thread t3 = new Thread(new Reader());
      t3.setName("Reader");
      t1.start();
      t2.start();
      t3.start();
      t1.join();
      t2.join();
      t3.join();
   }

   static class Reader implements Runnable {
      public void run() {
```

```java
      if(lock.isWriteLocked()) {
        System.out.println("Write Lock Present.");
      }
      lock.readLock().lock();
      try {
        Long duration = (long) (Math.random() * 10000);
        System.out.println(Thread.currentThread().getName()
          + " Time Taken " + (duration / 1000) + " seconds.");
        Thread.sleep(duration);
      } catch (InterruptedException e) {
        e.printStackTrace();
      } finally {
        System.out.println(Thread.currentThread().getName() +": "+ message );
        lock.readLock().unlock();
      }
    }
  }
}

static class WriterA implements Runnable {
  public void run() {
    lock.writeLock().lock();
    try {
      Long duration = (long) (Math.random() * 10000);
      System.out.println(Thread.currentThread().getName()
        + " Time Taken " + (duration / 1000) + " seconds.");
      Thread.sleep(duration);
    } catch (InterruptedException e) {
      e.printStackTrace();
    } finally {
      message = message.concat("a");
      lock.writeLock().unlock();
    }
  }
}

static class WriterB implements Runnable {
  public void run() {
    lock.writeLock().lock();
    try {
      Long duration = (long) (Math.random() * 10000);
      System.out.println(Thread.currentThread().getName()
        + " Time Taken " + (duration / 1000) + " seconds.");
```

```
            Thread.sleep(duration);
        } catch (InterruptedException e) {
            e.printStackTrace();
        } finally {
            message = message.concat("b");
            lock.writeLock().unlock();
        }
      }
    }
}
```

This will produce the following result.

Output

Writer A Time Taken 6 seconds.
Write Lock Present.
Writer B Time Taken 2 seconds.
Reader Time Taken 0 seconds.
Reader: aab

SUMMARY:

A thread executes a series of instructions. Every line of code that is executed is done so by a thread. In Java, the threads are executed independently to each other. Multithreading is vital to Java for two main reasons. First, multithreading enables you to write very efficient programs because it lets you utilize the idle time that is present in most programs. Most I/O devices, whether they be network ports, disk drives, or the keyboard, are much slower than the CPU. Thus, a program will often use a majority of its execution time waiting to send or receive information to or from a device. By using multithreading, your program can execute another task during this idle time. For example, while one part of your program is sending a file over the Internet, another part can be handling user interaction (such as mouse clicks or button presses), and still another can be buffering the next block of data to send.

The second reason that multithreading is important to Java relates to Java's eventhandling model. A program (such as an applet) must respond speedily to an event and then return. An event handler must not retain control of the CPU for an extended period of time.

10

APPLETS

10.1 INTRODUCTION TO APPLET

There are two kinds of Java programs, applications (also called stand-alone programs) and Applets. An **Applet** is a small Internet-based program that has the Graphical User Interface (GUI), written in the Java programming language.

Applets are designed to run inside a web browser or in applet viewer to facilitate the user to animate the graphics, play sound, and design the GUI components such as text box, button, and radio button. When applet arrives on the client, it has limited access to resources, so that it can produce arbitrary multimedia user interface and run complex computation without introducing the risk of viruses or breaching data integrity.

To create an applet, we extend the "java.applet.Applet" class And by overriding the methods of java.awt.Applet, new functionality can be placed into web pages.

Applets are compiled using javac compiler and it can be executed by using an appletviewer or by embedding the class file in the HTML (Hyper Text Markup Languege) file.

10.2 APPLET VS APPLICATION

Applets as previously described, are the small programs while applications are larger programs.

Applets don't have the main method while in an application execution starts with the main method.

Applets are designed just for handling the client site problems. while the java applications are designed to work with the client as well as server.

Applications are designed to exists in a secure area. while the applets are typically used.

Applications are not too small to embed into a html page so that the user can view the application in your browser. On the other hand applet have the accessibility criteria of the resources.

10.3 APPLET CLASS

The **java.applet** package is the smallest package in Java API(Application Programming Interface). The **Applet class** is the only class in the package. The Applet class has many methods that are used to display images, play audio files etc but it has no main() method. Some of them were explained below that give you the knowledge about Applets and their behavior.

init() : This method is used for whatever initializations are needed for your applet. Applets can have a default constructor, but it is better to perform all initializations in the init method instead of the default constructor.

start() :This method is automatically called after Java calls the init method. If this method is overwritten, code that needs to be executed every time that the user visits the browser page that contains this applet.

stop() : This method is automatically called when the user moves off the page where the applet sits. If your applet doesn't perform animation, play audio files, or perform calculations in a thread, you don't usually need to use this method.

destroy(): Java calls this method when the browser shuts down.

10.4 ADVANTAGES OF APPLET

Following are the advantages of a Java Applet:

1. The most important feature of an Applet is, It is truely platform independent so there is no need of making any changes in the code for different platform i.e. it is simple to make it work on Linux, Windows and Mac OS i.e. to make it cross platform.

2. The same applet can work on "all" installed versions of Java at the same time, rather than just the latest plug-in version only.

3. It can move the work from the server to the client, making a web solution more scalable with the number of users/clients.

4. The applet naturally supports the changing user state like figure positions on the chessboard.

5. Applets improves with use: after a first applet is run, the JVM is already running and starts quickly.

6. Applets can be used to provide dynamic user-interfaces and a variety of graphical effects for web pages.

10.5 APPLET LIFECYCLE

Every java Applet inherits a set of default behaviours from the Applet class. As a result, when an applet is loaded it undergoes a series of changes in its state.

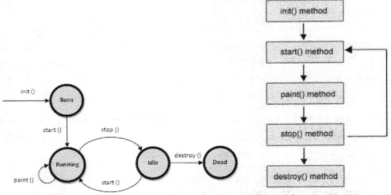

Figure: Life cycle of Applet

Following are the states in applets lifecycle.

1) Born or Initialisation state:

An applet begins its life when the web browser loads its classes and calls its init() method. This method is called exactly once in Applets lifecycle and is used to read applet parameters. Thus, in the init() method one should provide initialization code such as the initialization of variables.

Eg.　public void init()
```
{
        //initialisation
}
```

2) Running State:

Once the initialization is complete, the web browser will call the start() method in the applet. This method must called atleat once in the Applets lifecycle as the start() method can also be called if the Applet is in "Stoped" state. At this point the user can begin interacting with the applet.

Eg.　public void start()
```
{
        //Code
}
```

3) Stopped State:

The web browser will call the Applets stop() method, if the user moved to another web page while the applet was executing. So that the applet can take a breather while the user goes off and explores the web some more. The stop() method is called atleast once in Applets Lifecycle.

Eg.   publc void stop()
        {
                //Code
        }

4) Dead State:

Finally, if the user decides to quit the web browser, the web browser will free up system resources by killing the applet before it closes. To do so, it will call the applets destroy() method. One can override destroy() to perform one-time tasks upon program completion. for example, cleaning up threads which were started in the init() method.

Eg.   public void destroy()
        {
                // Code
        }

Note: If the user returns to the applet, the web browser will simply call the applet's start() method again and the user will be back into the program.

5) Display State :

Applet moves to the display state whenever it has to perform the output operations on the screen. This happens immediately after the applet enters into the running state. The paint() method is called to accomplish this task.

Eg.   public void paint(Graphics g)
        {
                //Display Statements
        }

10.6 MY FIRST APPLET
The following example is made simple enough to illustrate the essential use of Java applets through its java.applet package.

Example.
```
import java.awt.*;
import java.applet.*;
public class SimpleApplet extends Applet
{
        public void paint(Graphics g)
        {
```

```
            g.drawString("My First Applet",40,40);

    }
}
```

-> Save the file as **SimpleApplet.java**
-> Compile the file using **javac SimpleApplet.java**

Here is the illustration of the above example,

1. In the first line we imorts the Abstract Window Toolkit(AWT) classes as Applet interact with the user through the AWT, not through the console –based I/O classes. The AWT contains support for a window based graphical interface.

2. In the second line we import the Applet package, which contains the class "Applet". As every applet that we create is the subclass of Applet.

3. The next line declares the class SimpleApplet. This class must be declared in public, because it will be accessed by code that is outside the program.

4. Inside simpleApplet, paint() method is declared. This method is defined by the AWT and must be overridden by the Applet. Method paint() is called each time that the applet must redisplay its output.

   This paint() method has parameter of type " Graphics". This parameter contains the graphics context, which describes the graphics environment in which the applet is running. This context is used whenever output to the applet is required.

5. Inside paint() method is a call to drawstring(), which is a member of the Graphics class. This method output a String beginning at specified X, Y locations.

How to run an Applet?
There are two ways in which one can run an applet, as follows

1. Executing the applet within a java-compatible web browser.
2. Using an applet viewer, such as the standard SDK tool, "appletviewer". An applet viewer executes your applet in a window. This is generally the fastest and easiest way to test your applet.

To execute an applet in a web browser, you need to write a short HTML text file that contains the appropriate APPLET tag.

For above example it is <html>

<body>

<applet code="SimpleApplet.class" width=200 height=100>

</applet>

</body>

</html>

-> Save this code in text file with extension **.html** say **Myapplet.html.**

-> Compile the file using **javac SimpleApplet.java**

-> On successful compilation of SimpleApplet.java file, execute the this file using **appletviewer Myapplet.html** or just open this html file dirctly.

The output of above example appears as shown in the following figure:

OR

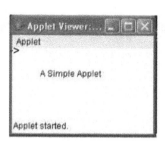
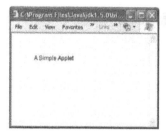

Insted of creating different text file for html code one can write above program as follows

```
import java.awt.*;
import java.applet.*;

/* <applet code="SimpleApplet" width=200 height=100> </applet>
*/
public class SimpleApplet extends Applet
{
        public void paint(Graphics g)
        {
                g.drawString("My First Applet",40,40);

        }
}
```

-> Save the file as **SimpleApplet.java**

-> Compile the file using **javac SimpleApplet.java**

-> On successful compilation, execute the this file using **appletviewer SimpleApplet.java**

The output remains same.

Building an applet code:

1. Applet code uses the series of two classes, namely Applet and Graphics from java class library.

2. Applet class which is contained in the java.applet package provides life and behaviour to the applet through its methods such as init(), start(), and paint().

3. When an applet is loaded, java automatically calls a series of applet class methods for starting, running and stopping the applet code.

4. The applet class therefore maintains the lifecycle of an applet.

5. The paint() method of the applet class, when it is called, actually display the rusult of applet code on the screen.

6. The output may be text, graphics or sound.

7. The paint() method, which requires a Graphics object as an argument, is defined as follows:

   public void paint(Graphics g)

8. This requires that the applet code imports the java.awt package that contains the Graphics class.

9. All output operations of an applet are performed using the methods defined in the Graphics class.

10.7 APPLET TAG

The Applet tag is used to start an applet from both HTML document and form applet viewer.

An applet viewer will execute each Applet tag that it finds in a separate window, while web browsers like Netscape Navigator,Internet Explorer and HotJava will allow many applets in a single page.

The <applet....> tag included in the body section of HTML file supplies the name of the applet to be loaded and tells the browser how much space the applet ruquires

The synatax for the standard Applet tag is as follows
```
<applet[codebase=codebaseURL] code="Applet file"
          [ALT="alternative text] [name=AppletInstanceName]
          Width=pixels height= pixels
          [align= alignment]
>
[<param name="Attributename" value ="Attribute value"] [<param
name="Attributename" value ="Attribute value"]
........

[HTML displayed in the absence of java] </applet>
```

Here is meaning of each peice of above code

Codebase: Codebase is an optional attribute that specifies the base URL of the applet code, which is the directory that will be searched for te applet's executable class file. The HTML document's URL directory is used as the CODEBASE if this attribute is not specified. The CODEBASE if this attribute is not specified. The CODEBASE does not have to be on the host from which the HTML document was read.

Code: code is required attribute that gives the name of the file containing the applets compiled .class file. This file is relative t the code base URL of the applet , which is the directory that the HTML file whs in or th edirectory indicated by the CODEBASE if set.

ALT : The ALT tag is an optional attribute used to specify a short text message that should be displayed if browser understand the APPLET tag but cant currently run java applet.

Name: Name is an optional attribute used to specify a name for the applet instance. Applets must be named in order for other applets on the same page to find them by name and communicate with them. To obtain an applet by name, use getAppet(), which is defined by the AppletContext interface.

Param name and value : The PARAM tag allows us to specify applet specific arguments in an HTML page. Applets access their attributes with the getParameter() method.

10.8 PASSING PARAMETERS TO APPLET

One can supply user-defined parameters to an applet using <param.....> tag. Each <param....> tag has a **name** attribute such as color,and a **value** attribute such as red. Inside the applet code, the applet can refer to that parameter by name to find its value. For e.g. the color of the text can be changed to red by an applet using a <param...> tag as follows

    <applet....>
        <param=color value = "red"> </applet>

Similarly we can change the text to be displayed by an applet by supplying new text to the applet through a <param....>tag as shown below.

    <param name=text value = "xyz" >

Passing a parameters to an applet is similar to passing parameters to main() method using command line arguments. To set up and handle parameters, we need to do two things.

Include appropriate <param.....> tags in the HTML document.

Provide code in the applet to pass these paraments.

Parameters are passed to an applet when it is loaded. We can define the init() method in the applet to get hold of the parameters defined in the <param> tags. This is done using the getparameter() method, which takes one string argument representing the name of the parameter and returns a string containing the value of that parameter.

10.9 TYPES OF APPLETS

As we can embed applet into web pages in two ways i.e. by writting our own applet and then embed into web pages. Or by downloading it from a remote computer system and then embed it into webpage.

An applet developed locally and stored in a local system is known as **local applet**. Therefore when webpage is trying to find local applet it doen not need the internet connection.

A **remote applte** is that which is developed by some one else and stored on a remote computer connected to the internet. If our system is connected to the internet then we can download it from remote computer and run it. In order to locate and load a remote applet, we must know the applet's address on the web. This address is known as Uniform Resourse locator(URL) and must be specified in applet's document.

10.10 EXAMPLES

Example 1 // Example to illustrate Applet Lifecycle

```
import java.awt.*; import
java.applet.*;
/* <applet code="AppletTest" width=200 height= 100> </applet>
*/
public class AppletTest extends Applet
{
        public void init()
        {
                System.out.println("Applet Initialised...");
                setBackground(Color.cyan);
        }
        public void start()
        {
                System.out.println("Applet Started....");
        }
        public void stop()
        {
                System.out.println("Applet Stoppen....");
        }
        public void destroy()
        {
                System.out.println("Applet Destryoed....");
        }
        public void paint(Graphics g)
        {
                g.drawString("Applet Text",200,400); showStatus("This
                is shown in Status.");
```

```
        }
}
```

-> Save the file as **AppletTest. Java**
-> Compile the file using **javac AppletTest.java**
-> On successful compilation, execute the file using
   appletviewer AppletTest.java

The output appers as shown in following figure :

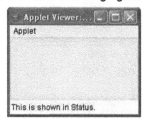

Example 2 // Example to illustrate Applet Lifecycle

```java
import java.awt.*; import
java.applet.*;
/* <applet code="Sample" width=200 height= 100> </applet>
*/

public class Sample extends Applet
{
        String msg;
        public void init()
        {
                setBackground(Color.cyan);
                setForeground(Color.red); msg = "Inside
                init()-";
        }

        public void start()
        {
                msg += "Inside start()-";
        }

        public void paint(Graphics g)
        {
                msg +="Inside paint()-"; g.drawString(msg,10,30);
                showStatus("This is shown at status");
        }
}
```

Save the file as **Sample. Java**
Compile the file using **javac Sample.java**
On successful compilation, execute the file using
appletviewer Sample.java

The output appers as shown in following figure :

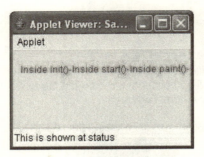

Example 3 // Example for passing parameters
import java.awt.*; import java.applet.*;
/* <applet code="ParamDemo" width=300 height= 80> <param name=fontName
   value=Courier>
   <param name=fontSize value=14> <param name=leading value
   = 2>
   <param name=accountEnabled value= true> </applet>
*/

```
public class ParamDemo extends Applet
{
        String fontName; int fontSize; float leading;
        boolean active;
public void start()
{
        String param; fontName=getParameter("fontName");
        if(fontName==null)
                fontName= "Not Found";
        param=getParameter("fontSize"); try
        {
                if(param!=null)
                fontSize=Integer.parseInt(param);
                else fontSize=0;
        }
catch(NumberFormatException e)
{
                fontSize=-1;
        }
param=getParameter("leading"); try
        {
                if(param!=null) leading=Float.valueOf(param).floatValue();
                else
                leading=0;
```

```
            }
      catch(NumberFormatException e)
      {
                  leading=0;
            }
      param=getParameter("accountEnabled"); if (param!=null)
      active =Boolean.valueOf(param).booleanValue();
      }
      public void paint(Graphics g)
      {
            g.drawString("Font Name." + fontName,0,10);
            g.drawString("Font Size." + fontSize,0,26);
            g.drawString("Leading." + leading,0,42);
            g.drawString("Account Active." + active,0,58);
      }
}
```

Save the file as **ParamDemo. Java**

Compile the file using **javac ParamDemo.java**

On successful compilation, execute the file using **a ppletviewer ParamDemo.java**

The output appers as shown in following figure :

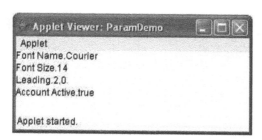

Example 4 // Example for getDocumentBase() & getCodeBase()
import java.awt.*; import

java.applet.*; import java.net.*;

/* <applet code="Bases" width=300 height= 50> </applet>
*/
public class Bases extends Applet

{
      public void paint(Graphics g)
      {

```
            String msg;
            URL url= getCodeBase();
            msg= "Code Base:" +url.toString();
            g.drawString(msg,10,20);
            url= getDocumentBase();
            msg= "Document Base:" +url.toString();
            g.drawString(msg,10,40);
        }
    }
```

Save the file as **Bases. Java**

Compile the file using **javac Bases.java**

On successful compilation, execute the file using **appletviewer Bases.java**

The output appers as shown in following figure :

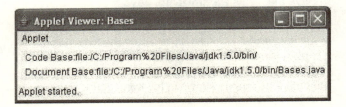

11

GRAPHICAL USER INTERFACE (GUI)

Unit Structure
Introduction
GUI Components
Interface and Classes of AWT Package
Layout managers
Methods of AWT

11.1 INTRODUCTION

A type of user interface item that allows people to interact with programs in more ways than typing such as computers and many hand-held devices such as mobile phones is called a **graphical user interface (GUI)** . A *GUI* offers graphical icons, and visual indicators, as opposed to text-based interfaces. This helps to develop more efficient programs that are easy to work with. The user can interact with the application without any problem.

The GUI application is created in three steps. These are:

Add components to Container objects to make your GUI.
Then you need to setup event handlers for the user interaction with GUI.
Explicitly display the GUI for application.

11.2 GUI COMPONENTS

It is visual object and the user interacts with this object via a mouse or a keyboard. Components included, can be actually seen on the screen, such as, buttons, labels etc. Any operation that is common to all GUI components are found in class Component. Different components are available in the Java AWT (Abstract Window Toolkit)package for developing user interface for your program.

A class library is provided by the Java programming language which is known as Abstract Window Toolkit (AWT). The Abstract Window Toolkit (AWT) contains several graphical widgets which can be added and positioned to the display area with a layout manager.

AWT is a powerful concept in JAVA. AWT is basically used to develop for GUI application building. AWT is platform dependant. That means your **.class** file after the program compilation is platform independent but the look of your GUI application is platform dependant. AWT copies GUI component from local macines operating system. That means your applications look will differ in MAC operating system, as you have seen in WINDOWS operating system.

11.3 INTERFACE AND CLASSES OF AWT PACKAGE:

Some of the Classes Interfaces of AWT package are explained below

Interfaces	Descriptions
ActionEvent	This interface is used for handling events.
Adjustable	This interface takes numeric value to adjust within the bounded range.
Composite	This interface defines methods to draw a graphical area. It combines a shape, text, or image etc.
CompositeContext	This interface allows the existence of several contexts simultaneously for a single composite object. It handles the state of the operations.
ItemSelectable	This interface is used for maintaining zero or more selection for items from the item list.
KeyEventDispatcher	The KeyEventDispatcher implements the current KeyboardFocusManager and it receives KeyEvents before dispatching their targets.
KeyEventPostProcessor	This interface also implements the current KeyboardFocusManager. The KeyboardFocusManager receives the KeyEvents after that dispatching their targets.
LayoutManager	It defines the interface class and it has layout containers.
LayoutManager2	This is the interface extends from the LayoutManager and is subinterface of that.
MenuContainer	This interface has all menu containers.
Paint	This interface is used to color pattern. It used for the Graphics2D operations.
PaintContext	This interface also used the color pattern. It provides an important color for the Graphics2D operation and uses the ColorModel.
PaintGraphics	This interface provides print a graphics

	context for a page.
Shape	This interface used for represent the geometric shapes.
Stroke	This interface allows the Graphics2D object and contains the shapes to outline or stylistic representation of outline.
Transparency	This interface defines the transparency mode for implementing classes.

Class hierarchy of AWT classes can be given as follows.

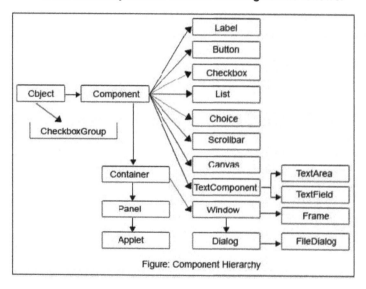

Figure: Component Hierarchy

11.3.1 Labels:

This is the simplest component of Java Abstract Window Toolkit. This component is generally used to show the text or string in your application and label never perform any type of action.

Syntax for defining the label only and with justification:
Label label_name = new Label ("This is the label text.");
above code simply represents the text for the label.

Label label_name = new Label ("This is the label text. " , Label.CENTER);

Justification of label can be left, right or centered. Above declaration used the center justification of the label using the Label.CENTER.

Example for Label.

```
import java.awt.*;
import java.applet.Applet;
 /*<applet code="LabelTest" width=200 height=100> </applet>
*/
public class LabelTest extends Applet
{
  public void init()
  {
    add(new Label("A label")); // right justify
    next label
    add(new Label("Another label", Label.RIGHT));
    }
}
```

Save the file as **LabelTest. Java**

Compile the file using **javac LabelTest.java**
On successful compilation, execute the file using
appletviewer LabelTest.java

The output appers as shown in following figure :

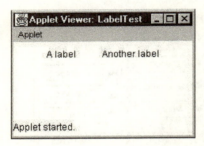

11.3.2 Buttons:

This is the component of Java Abstract Window Toolkit and is used to trigger actions and other events required for your application. The syntax of defining the button is as follows:

Button button_name = new Button ("This is the label of the button.");

You can change the Button's label or get the label's text by using the Button.setLabel (String) and Button.getLabel () method. Buttons are added to its container using the, add (button_name) method.

Example for Buttons:-

```
import java.awt.*;
import java.applet.Applet;
/*<applet code="ButtonTest" width=200 height=100> </applet>
* /
public class ButtonTest extends Applet
{
public void init()
        {
        Button button = new Button ("OK"); add (button);
        }
 }
```

Save the file as **ButtonTest. Java**
Compile the file using **javac ButtonTest.java**
On successful compilation, execute the file using **appletviewer ButtonTest.java**

The output appers as shown in following figure :

Note that in the above example there is no event handling added; pressing the button will not do anything.

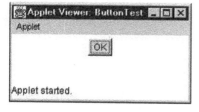

11.3.3 Check Boxes:

This component of Java AWT allows you to create check boxes in your applications. The syntax of the definition of Checkbox is as follows:

Checkbox checkbox_name = new Checkbox ("Optional check box 1", false);

Above code constructs the unchecked Checkbox by passing the boolean valued argument *false* with the Checkbox label through the Checkbox() constructor. Defined Checkbox is added to its container using add (checkbox_name) method. You can change and get the checkbox's label using the setLabel (String) and getLabel () method. You can also set and get the state of the checkbox using the setState (boolean) and getState () method provided by the Checkbox class.

Example for Check Boxes:-

```java
import java.awt.*;
import java.applet.Applet;
/*<applet code="CheckboxTest" width=200 height=100> </applet>
*
public class CheckboxTest extends Applet
{
        public void init()
        {
           Checkbox m = new Checkbox ("Allow Mixed Case"); add (m);
        }
}
```

Save the file as **CheckboxTest. Java**

Compile the file using **javac CheckboxTest.java**

On successful compilation, execute the file using **appletviewer CheckboxTest.java**

The output appers as shown in following figure :

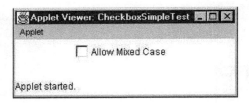

11.3.4 Radio Button:

Radio buttons are a bunch of option boxes in a group. Only one of then can be checked at a time. This is useful if you need to give the user a few options where only one will apply. This is the special case of the Checkbox component of Java AWT package. This is used as a group of checkboxes whos group name is same. Only one Checkbox from a Checkbox Group can be selected at a time.

Syntax for creating radio buttons is as follows:

CheckboxGroup chkboxgp = new CheckboxGroup (); add (new Checkbox ("chkboxname", chkboxgp, value);

"Value" in the second statement can only be true or false.If you mention more than one true valued for checkboxes then your program takes the last true and shows the last check box as checked.

Example for Radio Buttons.

```
import java.awt.*;
import java.applet.Applet;
/*<applet code="Rbutton" width=200 height=100> </applet>
*/
public class Rbutton extends Applet
{
   public void init()
        {
        CheckboxGroup chkgp = new CheckboxGroup (); add (new
        Checkbox ("One", chkgp, false));
        add (new Checkbox ("Two", chkgp, false)); add (new
        Checkbox ("Three",chkgp, false));

        }
     }
```

In the above code we are making three check boxes with the label "One", "Two" and "Three".

Save the file as **Rbutton. Java**
Compile the file using **javac Rbutton.java**
On successful compilation, execute the file using
appletviewer Rbutton.java

The output appers as shown in following figure :

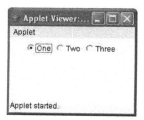

11.3.5 Text Area:

This is the text container component of Java AWT package. The Text Area contains plain text. TextArea can be declared as follows:

TextArea txtArea_name = new TextArea ();

You can make the Text Area editable or not using the setEditable (boolean) method. If you pass the boolean valued argument *false* then the text area will be non-editable otherwise it will be editable. The text area is by default in editable mode. Texts are set in the text area using the setText (string) method of the TextArea class.

Example for Text Area:-

```
import java.awt.*;
import java.applet.Applet;
/*<applet code="TAreaTest" width=200 height=100> </applet>
*/
public class TAreaTest extends Applet
{
        TextArea disp; public void init()
        {
          disp = new TextArea("Code goes here", 10, 30); add (disp);
        }
}
```

Save the file as **TAreaTest. Java**
Compile the file using **javac TAreaTest.java**
On successful compilation, execute the file using
appletviewer TAreaTest.java

The output appers as shown in following figure :

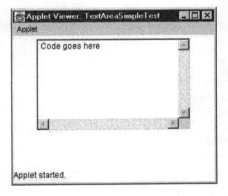

11.3.6 Text Field:

This is also the text container component of Java AWT package. This component contains single line and limited text information. This is declared as follows:

TextField txtfield = new TextField (20);

You can fix the number of columns in the text field by specifying the number in the constructor. In the above code we have fixed the number of columns to 20.

A displayed label object is known as the Label. Most of the times label is used to demonstrate the significance of the other parts of the GUI. It helps to display the functioning of the next text field. A label is also restricted to a single line of text as a button.

Example for Text Field:-

```
import java.awt.*;
import java.applet.Applet;
/*<applet code="TFieldTest" width=200 height=100> </applet>
*/

public class TFieldTest extends Applet
{
        public void init()
        {
          TextField f1 =
            new TextField("type something"); add(f1);
          }
}
```

Save the file as **TFieldTest. Java**

Compile the file using **javac TFieldTest.java**
On successful compilation, execute the file using
appletviewer TFieldTest.java

The output appers as shown in following figure :

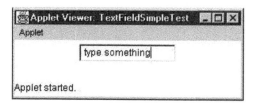

159

11.3.7 Scrollbar

Scrollbar is represented by a "slider" widget. The characteristics of it are specified by integer values which are being set at the time of scrollbar construction. Both the types of Sliders are available i.e. horizontal and vertical.

The example below shows the code for the scrollbar construction. The subtraction of scrollbar width from the maximum setting gives the maximum value of the Scrollbar. In the program code, '0' is the <<<<<<< scrollbar.shtml initial value of the scrollbar, '8' is the width of the scrollbar.

Example for Scrollbar

```
import java.awt.*;
import java.applet.Applet;
 /*<applet code="ScrollbarDemo" width=200 height=100> </applet>
*/
public class ScrollbarDemo extends Applet
{
  public void init()
  {
    Scrollbar sb = new Scrollbar (Scrollbar.VERTICAL, 0, 8, 100, 100);
    add(sb);
  }
}
```

Save the file as **ScrollbarDemo. Java**
Compile the file using **javac ScrollbarDemo.java**
On successful compilation, execute the file using
appletviewer ScrollbarDemo.java

The output appers as shown in following figure :

11.3.8 Panels

A panel is an object which holds other objects. It's just a container to organize and arrange your GUI better. Once, you learn about Layout Managers you'll see why panels are a useful tool. For now, just know that they're useful. Here's an example of a set of buttons added into a panel:
Panel myPanel = new Panel();
myPanel.add(helloButton);
myPanel.add(goodbyeButton);
add(myPanel);

It looks no different than if you just added the buttons regularly, but you'll see why you might want to use panels later on...
This is what it looks like:

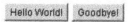

11.4 LAYOUT MANAGERS

The layout manager are a set of classes that implement the **java.AWT.LayoutManager** interface and help to position the components in a container. The interface takes a task of laying out the child components in the container. The task is achieved by resizing and moving the child components. The advantages of this type of mechanism is that when the container is resized the layout manager automatically updates the interface

The basic layout managers includes:
FlowLayout : It is a simple layout manager that works like a word processor. It is also the default Layout manager for the panel. The flow layout lays out components linewise from left to right.

FlowLaout can be created using following constructors

FlowLaout() : Constructs a new layout with centered alignment, leaving a vertical and horizontal gap.

FlowLayout(int aling, int vgap, int hgap) : Constructs a new flowlayout with the alignment specified, leaving a vertical and horizontal gap as specified.

Various methods can be used alog with the flow layout. For eg.
getAlignment(), getHgap(), getAlignment(int align) etc.

Example for Flow Layout
import java.awt.*; import
java.awt.event.*;
class FlowDemo extends Frame
{

```
Button b1 = new Button("one"); Button b2 =
new Button("two"); public FlowDemo(String
s)
{
super(s);
setSize(400,400);
setLayout(new FlowLayout(FlowLayout.LEFT));
addWindowListener(new WindowAdapter()
{
public void windowClosing(WindowEvent e)
{
System.exit(0);
}
});
add(b1);
add(b2);
}
public static void main(String arg[])
{
Frame f=new Frame(); f.show();
}
}
```

Save the file as **FlowDemo. Java**
Compile the file using **javac FlowDemo.java**
On successful compilation, execute the file using **java FlowDemo.java**

Grid Layout : It lays out components in a way very similar to spred sheet (rows and columns). Specifying the number of rows and columns in grid creates the Grid layout.

Grid Layout can be created using following constructors

GridLayout() : Creates a grid layout with a default of one column per component in a single row.

GridLayout(int rows, int cols, int hgap, int vgap) : Creates a grid layout with the specified rows and columns and specified horizontal and vertical gaps.

Various methods can be used alog with the Grid layout. For eg. getColumns(), getRows(), geHgap(), getVgap() etc.

Example for Grid Layout
import java.applet.Applet; import
java.awt.*;

```java
public class Grid1 extends Applet {
  LayoutManager Layout;
  Button [ ] Buttons;
  public Grid1 () { int i;
    Layout = new GridLayout (3, 2); setLayout
    (Layout);
    Buttons = new Button [5]; for (i = 0; i <
    5; ++i) {
      Buttons[i] = new Button (); Buttons[i].setLabel
      ("Button " + (i + 1)); add (Buttons[i]);
    }
  }
}
```

Save the file as **Grid1. Java**
Compile the file using **javac Grid1.java**
On successful compilation, execute the file using
appletviewer Grid1.java

The output appers as shown in following figure :

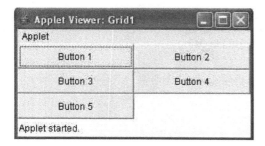

BorderLayout : It is the class that enables specification, i.e. where on the border of container each component should be placed. All areas need not be filled. The size of the areas will depend on the components they contain.

Border Layout can be created using following constructors a.
BorderLayout() : It creates a new border layout with no
gap between the components.

BorderLayout(int hgap, int vgap) : It creates a border layout with the specified horizontal and vertical gap between components.

Various methods can be used alog with the Border layout. For eg. getHgap(), getVgap(), setHgap(int hgap), setVgap(int vgap)

Example for Border Layout
import java.awt.*;
import java.applet.*;
import java.util.*;

```
/*<applet code="BorderDemo" width=300 height=100>
</applet>
*/
public class BorderDemo extends Applet

{

public void init()

{

setLayout(new BorderLayout());
add(new Button("This across the top"),BorderLayout.NORTH);
add(new Button("The Footer message might go here"),BorderLayout.SOUTH);
add(new Button("Right"),BorderLayout.EAST); add(new

Button("Left"),BorderLayout.WEST);

String msg=" This is border layout";

add(new TextArea(msg),BorderLayout.CENTER); add(new

Button("new"),BorderLayout.CENTER);

}

}
```

Save the file as **BorderDemo. Java**
Compile the file using **javac BorderDemo.java**
On successful compilation, execute the file using
appletviewer BorderDemo.java

The output appers as shown in following figure :

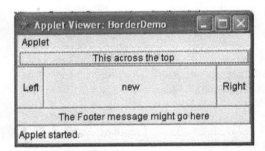

11.5 METHODS OF AWT
The common methods of AWT components are as follow:

getLocation () - This method is used to get position of the component, as a Point. The usage of the method is shown below.

Point p = someComponent.getLocation (); int x = p.x;
int y = p.y;

the x and y parts of the location can be easily accessed by using getX () and getY (). It is always efficient to use getX () and getY () methods.

For example,
int x = someComponent.getX(); int y = someComponent.getY();

getLocationOnScreen () - This method is used to get the position of the upper-left corner of the screen of the component, as a Point. The usage of the method is shown below.

Point p = someComponent.getLocationOnScreen (); int x = p.x;
int y = p.y;

It is always advisable to use getLocation () method (if working on Java 2 platform).

getBounds () - This method is used to get the current bounding Rectangle of component. The usage of the method is shown below.
Rectangle r = someComponent.getBounds (); int height = r.height;
int width = r.width; int x = r.x;
int y = r.y;

if you need a Rectangle object then the efficient way is to use getX (), getY(), getWidth(), and getHeight() methods.

getSize () - This method is used to get the current size of component, as a Dimension. The usage of the method is shown below.
Dimension d = someComponent.getSize (); int height = d.height;
int width = d.width;

use getWidth () and getHeight () methods to directly access the width and height. You can also use getSize () if you require a Dimension object.
For Example,
int height = someComponent.getHeight();
int width = someComponent.getWidth();

setBackground(Color)/setForeground(Color) - This method is used to change the background/foreground colors of the component

setFont (Font) - This method is used to change the font of text within a component.

setVisible (boolean) - This method is used for the visibility state of the component. The component appears on the screen if setVisible () is set to true and if it's set to false then the component will not appear on the screen. Furthermore, if we mark the component as not visible then the component will disappear while reserving its space in the GUI.

setEnabled (boolean) - This method is used to toggle the state of the component. The component will appear if set to true and it will also react to the user. ON the contrary, if set to false then the component will not appear hence no user interaction will be there.

As discussed earlier a container is a component that can be nested. The most widely used Panel is the Class Panel which can be extended further to partition GUIs. There is a Panel which is used for running the programs. This Panel is known as Class Applet which is used for running the programs within the Browser.

Common Container Methods:-

All the subclasses of the Container class inherit the behavior of more than 50 common methods of Container. These subclasses of the container mostly override the method of component. Some of the methods of container which are most widely used are as follow:

```
getComponents (); add();
getComponentCount();
getComponent(int);
```

ScrollPane:-

The ScrollPane container provides an automatic scrolling of any larger component introduced with the 1.1 release of the Java Runtime Environment (JRE). Any image which is bigger in size for the display area or a bunch of spreadsheet cells is considered as a large object. Moreover there is no LayoutManager for a ScrollPane because only a single object exists within it. However, the mechanism of Event Handling is being managed for scrolling.

The example below shows the Scrollpane. This scrollpane demonstrates the scrolling of the large image. In the program code below, first of all we have created a scrollpane by creating its object, and then we have passed the parameter of image in it. We have also set the border layout as centre, as shown.

Example for Scroll Pane
```
import java.awt.*;
import java.applet.*;
 /*<applet code="ScrollingImageDemo" width=200 height=100> </applet>
*/
class Scrollpane extends Component { private
  Image image;
  public Scrollpane(Image m)
{
   image = m;
 }
 public void paint(Graphics g)
 {
   if (image != null) g.drawImage(image, 0, 0,
     this);
```

```
  }
}
```

public class ScrollingImageDemo extends Applet

```
{
  public void init()
  {
    setLayout(new BorderLayout());
    ScrollPane SC = new ScrollPane(ScrollPane.SCROLLBARS_AL WAYS);

    Image mg = getImage(getCodeBase(), "cute-puppy.gif"); SC.add(new
    Scrollpane(mg));
    add(SC, BorderLayout.CENTER);
  }
}
```

-> Save the file as **ScrollingImageDemo. Java**

-> Compile the file using **javac ScrollingImageDemo.java**
-> On successful compilation, execute the file using
appletviewer ScrollingImageDemo.java

The output appers as shown in following figure :

EVENT HANDLING

Unit Structure
Introduction
Event
Event Source
Event Classes
Event Listener
Examples
Handling Windows Events
Adapter Classes

12.1 INTRODUCTION

Writing an applet that responds to user input, introduces us to event handling. We can make our applet respond to user input by overriding event handler methods in our applet. There are a variety of event handler methods which we will see further.

Each event must return a Boolean value (true or false), indicating whether the event should be made available to other event handlers. If you've processed an event (for example, keyDown) you might record the value, and return true to show that no other handlers should receive the event. If, however, your custom edit box can't process the character, it may want to return false to signal that other components (the panel or applet in which the component is hosted) should process it.

12.2 EVENT:

An **Event** is an object that describes a state change in a source. It can be generated as a consequence of a person interacting with the elements in a GUI. Some of the activities that cause events to be generated are pressing a button, entering a character via the keyboard, selecting an item in a list, and clicking the mouse.

Events may also occur that are not directly caused by interactions with user interface. For e.g. an event may be generated when a timer expires, a counter exceeds a value, a software or hardware failure occurs, or an operation is completed.

12.3 EVENT SOURCE:

An **event source** is the object that generates an event. This occurs when the internal state of that object changes in some way. Sources may generate more than one type of event. A source may register listeners in order for the listeners to receive notifications about a specific type of event. Each type of event has its own registration method. Example if you click a button an . ActionEvent Object is generated. The object of the ActionEvent class contains information about the event.

In addition to GUI elements, other components such as an Applet, can generate Events. For e.g. you receive key and mouse events from an Applet.

Following is the table to describe some of the Event Sources.

Event Sources	Description
Button	Generates action events when the button is pressed.
	box is selected or deselected.
List	Generates action events when an item is double-clicked; generates item events when an item is selected or deselected.
Choice	Generates item events when the choice is changed.
MenuItem	Generates action events when a menu item is selected; generates item events when a checkable menu item is selected or deselected.
Scrollbar	Generates adjustment events when the scrollbar is manipulated.
Text components	Generates text events when the user enters a character.
Window	Generates window events when a window is activated, closed , deactivated, deiconified, iconified, opened, or quit.

12.4 EVENT CLASSES

The **'EventObject'** class is at the top of the event class hierarchy. It belongs to the java.util package. While most of the other event classes are present in java.awt.event package. The **getSource()** method of the EventObject class returns the object that initiated the event. The **getId ()** method returns the nature of the event. For example, if a mouse event occurs, you can find out whether the event was click, a press, a move or release from the event object.

Following is the table to describe the Event Classes.

Event Class	Discription
ActionEvent	A semantic event which indicates that a component-defined action occurred.
AdjustmentEvent	The adjustment event emitted by Adjustable objects.
ComponentEvent	A low-level event which indicates that a component moved, changed size, or changed visibility (also, the root class for the other component-level events).
ContainerEvent	A low-level event which indicates that a container's contents changed because a component was added or removed.
InputEvent	The root event class for all component-level input events.
ItemEvent	A semantic event which indicates that an item was selected or deselected.
KeyEvent	An event which indicates that a keystroke occurred in a component.
MouseEvent	An event which indicates that a mouse action occurred in a component.
MouseWheelEvent	An event which indicates that the mouse wheel was rotated in a component.
PaintEvent	The component-level paint event.
TextEvent	A semantic event which indicates that an object's text changed.
WindowEvent	A low-level event that indicates that a window has changed its status.

12.5 EVENT LISTENER:

These are objects that define methods to handle certain type of events. An event source (for example a PushButton) can generate one or more type of events, and maintain a list of event listeners for each type of event. An event source can register listeners by calling addXListener type of methods. For example a Button may register an object for handling ActionEvent by calling addActionListener. This object would then need to implement the listener interface corresponding to ActionEvent, which is ActionListener.

So to set up the processing of events the following tasks must be done.

1. For the GUI component (like pushbutton) associate a listener object class with the component by calling a method of type addXListener (See table below for list of methods).

2. Define this listener object. It must implement the corresponding interface. The name of interface is of type EventListener. Table below gives list of event listeners.

3. The object must define all the methods defined in the interface it is implementing. See table for the list of Event Listener methods defined in each Event Listener interface

Interface	Description
ActionListener	Define one method to receive action events
AdjustmentListener	Defines one method to receive adjustment events.
ComponentListener	Defines four methods to recognize when a component is hidden, moved, resized, or shown.
ContainerListener	Defines two methods to recognize when a component is added to or removed from a container.
Focus Listener	Defines two methods to recognize when a component gains or loses keyboard focus.
ItemListener	Defines one method to recognize when the state of an item is changes.
KeyListener	Defines 3 methods to recognize when a key is pressed, released, or typed.
MouseListener	Defines 5 methods to recognize when the mouse is clicked, enters a component, exits a component, is pressed, or is released
MouseMotionListener	Defines two methods to recognize when the mouse is dragged or moved.
MouseWheelListener	Defines one method to recognize when mouse wheel is moved.
TextListener	Defines one method to recognize when a text value changes.
WindowFocusListener	Defines two methods to recognize when window gains or loses focus.
WindowListner	Defines 7 methods to recognize when a window is activated, closed, deactivated,deiconified,iconified, opened, or quit.

12.6 EXAMPLES

1) Example for MouseEvents & MouseListener

```java
import java.awt.*; import
java.awt.event.*; import
java.applet.*;

/*<applet code= "mouseEvent" width=400 height=300> </applet?
*/
public class mouseEvent extends Applet implements
MouseListener, MouseMotionListener
{
        public void init ()
        {
                addMouseListener (this); addMouseMotionListener (this);
        }
        public void mouseClicked(MouseEvent e)
        {
                showStatus ("Mouse has been clicked at " + e.getX()+ "," + e.getY());
        }

        public void mouseEntered (MouseEvent e)
        {
        showStatus ("Mouse has been Entered at " + e.getX()+ "," + e.getY());
        // For loop: to make sure mouse entered is on status bar for a few sec
        for (int i= 0; i<1000000; i++);
        }
        public void mouseExited (MouseEvent e)
        {
        showStatus ("Mouse has been Exited at " + e.getX()+ "," + e.getY());
        }

        public void mousePressed (MouseEvent e)
        {
        showStatus ("Mouse pressed at " + e.getX()+ "," +e.getY());
        }

        public void mouseReleased (MouseEvent e)
        {
        showStatus ("Mouse released at " + e.getX()+ "," +e.getY());
        }
```

```java
        public void mouseDragged (MouseEvent e)
        {
        showStatus ("Mouse dragged at " + e.getX()+ "," +e.getY());
        }

        public void mouseMoved(MouseEvent e)
        {
        showStatus ("Mouse moved at " + e.getX()+ "," +e.getY());
        }
        //public void paint(Graphics g)
        {
        //g.drawString(msg, e.getX(), e.getY());
        }
}
```

Save the file as **mouseEvent. Java**

Compile the file using **javac mouseEvent.java**

On successful compilation, execute the file using **appletviewer mouseEvent.java**

The output appers as shown in following figure :

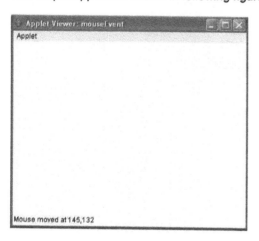

2) Example for Key events and KeyListener.

```java
import java.awt.*;
import java.awt.event.*;
import java.applet.*;
/*<applet code="keyTest" width =400 height=300> </applet>
*/
public class keyTest extends Applet implements KeyListener
{
        public void init()
        {
```

```
                Label lab = new Label ("Enter Characters :"); add (lab);
                TextField tf = new TextField (20); add (tf);
                tf.addKeyListener(this);
     }
        public void keyPressed(KeyEvent e)
        {
        showStatus("key Down");
        }
        public void keyReleased(KeyEvent e)
        {
        showStatus("key Up");
        }
        public void keyTyped(KeyEvent e)
        {
                showStatus(" Recently typed characters are : " + e.getKeyChar());
        }
}
```

Save the file as **keyTest. Java**
Compile the file using **javac keyTest.java**
On successful compilation, execute the file using
appletviewer keyTest.java

The output appers as shown in following figure :

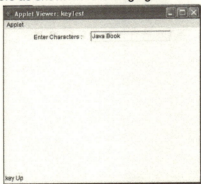

3) Example for Button Event and Action Listener

```
import java.awt.*; import
java.awt.event.*;
import java.applet.Applet;
/*
<applet code = "ButtonEvent" height = 400 width = 400> </applet>
*/
public class ButtonEvent extends Applet implements ActionListener
{
 Button b;
```

```
        public void init()
        {
                b = new Button("Click me");
                b.addActionListener(this); add (b);
        }

        public void actionPerformed (ActionEvent e)
        {
                /*If the target of the event was our
                Button. In this example, the check is not
                Truly necessary as we only listen to
                A single button */

        if(e.getSource () == b)
        {
                getGraphics().drawString("OUCH Buddy",20,20);
        }
        }
}
```

Save the file as **ButtonEvent. Java**
Compile the file using **javac ButtonEvent.java**
On successful compilation, execute the file using
appletviewer ButtonEvent.java

The output appers as shown in following figure :

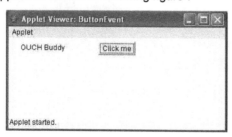

12.7 HANDLING WINDOWS EVENTS:

When you use interfaces for creating listeners, the listener class has to override all the methods that are declared in the interface. Some of the interfaces have only one method, whereas others(windowListener) have many. So even if you want to handle only a single event, you have to override all the methods. To overcome this, the event packages provide seven adapter classes, which we will see shortly. Now coming back to handle window-related events, you need to register the listener object that implements the windowListener interface. The WindowListener interface contains a set of methods that are used to handle window events.

Category	Event	Method
Windows Events	The user clicks on the cross button.	void windowClosing (WindowEvent e)
	The window opened for the first time.	void windowOpened (WindowEvent e)
	The window is activated.	void windowActivated (WindowEvent e)
	The window is deactivated.	void windowDeactivated (WindowEvent e)
	The window is closed.	void windowClosed (WindowEvent e)
	The window is minimized	void windowIconified (WindowEvent e)
	The window maximized	void windowDeiconified (WindowEvent e)

example for Window Events

```
import java.awt.*;
import java.awt.event.*;
 Class OurWindowListener implements windowListener
{
    //Event handler for the window closing event public void
    windowClosing (windowEvent we)
    {
            System.exit(0);
    }
    public void windowClosed (windowEvent we)
    {

    }
    public void windowOpened (windowEvent we)
    {
    }
    public void windowActivated (windowEvent we)
    {

    }
     public void windowDeactivated (windowEvent we)
    {

    }
    public void windowIconified (windowEvent we)
    {

    }
    public void windowDeiconified (windowEvent we)
    {

    }
```

```
}
public class MyFrame extends Frame
{
    Button b1;
    // Main Method
    public static void main (String arg[])
    {
        MyFrame f = new MyFrame();
    }
    //Constructor for the event derived class public MyFrame()
    {
        Super ("Windows Events-Title");
        b1 = new button("Click Me");
        //place the button object on the window add("center",b1);

        //Register the listener for the button

            ButtonListener listen = new ButtonListener();
            b1.addActionListener(listen);

        //Register a listener for the window.
            OurWindowListener wlisten = new OurWindowListener();
            addWindowListener(wlisten);

        //display the window in a specific size
            setVisible(true);
            setSize(200,200);
    }//end of frame class


//The Listener Class
    Class ButtonListener implements ActionListener
    {
        //Definition for ActionPerformed() method
        public void ActionPerformed(ActionEvent evt)
        {
            Button source = (Button)evt.getSource();
            Source.setLabel("Button Clicked, Buddy!");
        }
    }
}
```

In the above example MyFrame class makes a call to the addWindowListener() method, which registers object for the window. This enables the application to handle all the window-related events. When the user interacts with the application by clicking close button, maximizing or minimizing a WindowEvent object is created and delegated to the pre-registered listener of the window. Subsequently the designated event-handler is called.

In the above example, the class OurWindowListener has methods that do not contain any code. This is because the windowListener interface contains declarations for all these methods forcing you to override them.

12.8 ADAPTER CLASSES:

Java provides us with adapter classes that implement the corresponding listener interfaces containing one or more methods. The methods in these classes are empty. The Listener class that you define can extend the Adapter class and override the methods that you need. The adapter class used for WindowListener interface is the WindowAdapter class.

So you can simplify the above code (example 2) using Adapter class in the following manner:

Example: Save as MyFrames.java and complie.
import java.awt.*; import

java.awt.event.*;

Class MyFrames extends frame

{

    public static void main(String arg[])

    {

        MyFrames f = new MyFrames();

    }

    //constructor of the Frame derived class public

    MyFrames

    {

        //Register the Listener for the window super("The

        Window Adapter Sample");

        MyWindowListener mlisten = new MyWindowListener();

        addWindowListener(mlisten);

        setVisible(true);

    }

}

Class MyWindowListener extends WindowAdapter

{

    //event handler for windows closing event public void

    windowClosing(WindowEvent we)

```
    {
        MyFrames f;
        f = (MyFrames)we.getSource();
        f.dispose();
        System.exit(0);
    }
}
```

The Following is a list of Adapter classes and Listener Interfaces In Java:

Event Category	Interface Name	Adapter Name	Method
Window	Window Listener	Window Adapter	Void windowClosing (WindowEvent e)
			Void windowOpened (WindowEvent e)
			Void windowActivated (WindowEvent e)
			Void windowDeactivated (WindowEvent e)
			Void windowClosed (WindowEvent e)
			Void windowIconified (WindowEvent e)
			Void windowDeiconified (WindowEvent e)
Action	ActionListener		Void actionPerformed (ActionEvent e)
Item	ItemListener		Void itemStateChanged (ItemEvent e)
Mouse Motion	MouseMotion Listener	MouseMotion Adapter	Void mouseDragged (MouseEvent e)
			Void mouseMoved (MouseEvent e)
Mouse Button	MouseListener	MouseAdapter	Void mousePressed
			Void mouseEntered (MouseEvent e)
			Void mouseClicked (MouseEvent e)
			Void mouseExited (MouseEvent e)
Key	KeyListener	KeyAdapter	Void keyPressed (KeyEvent e)
			Void keyReleased (KeyEvent e)
			Void keyTyped(KeyEvent e)
Focus	FocusListener		Void focusGained (FocusEvent e)
			Void focusLost (FocusEvent e)
Component	ComponentListener	Component Adapter	Void componentMoved (ComponentEvent e)
			Void componentResized(ComponentEvent e)
			Void componentHidden (ComponentEvent e)
			Void componentShown (ComponentEvent e)

Inner classes are classes that are declared within other classes. They are also knows as nested classes and provide additional clarity to the program. The scope of the inner class is limited to the class that encloses it. The object of the inner class can access the members of the outer class. While the outer class can access the members of the inner class through an object of the inner class.

Syntax:
```
class
{
    class
    {
    }
    //other attributes and methods
}
```

Example: Save as MyFrame.java then compile and excute the program.
import java.awt.*; import

java.awt.event.*;

Class MyFrame extends Frame

```
{
    //inner class declaration
    class MyWindowListener extends MyAdapter
    {
        //event handler for windows closing event public void
        windowClosing(WindowEvent w)
        {
            MyFrame frm;
            frm = (MyFrames)w.getSource();
            frm.dispose();
            System.exit(0);
        }
    }

    public static void main(String arg[])
    {
        MyFrame frm = new MyFrame();
    }

    //constructor of the Frame class public
    MyFrames
    {
        //Register the Listener for the window super("Illustration For
        Inner or Nested Classes"); //creating an object of inner class
```

```
        MyWindowListener wlisten = new MyWindowListener();
        addWindowListener(wlisten);
        setVisible(true);
        setSize(100,100);
    }
}
```

The above example code declares an object of the inner class in the constructor of an outer class. To create an object of the inner class from an unrelated class, you can use the new operator as if it were a member of the outer class.

Example:
```
MyFrame frame = new MyFrame("Title");
Frame.MyWindowsListener listen = new
MyFrame().MyWindowListener();
```
You can create a class inside a method. The methods of the inner class can have access to the variables define in the method containing them. Inner class must be declared after the declaration of the variables of the method so those variables are accessible to the inner class.

Example: Save As RadioTest.java, Compile And View Using Appletviewer

In this Applet example we examine MouseAdapters, and its methods like mouseClicked(). Plus ItemListener interface implementation and itemStateChanged() method and use getItem() method to display the item the user as selected in the Applet's status bar using the showStatus()method. We will use interface components like checkbox, which are of two types-exclusive checkboxes (which means only one among the group can be selected) also called Radio Buttons. We also use non-inclusive checkboxes, which can be selected independently. The Choice class implements the pop-up menu that allows users to select items from a menu. This UI component dispalys the currently selected item with a arrow to its right.

```
/*
<applet code = "RadioTest.class" height = 300 width = 300 > </applet>
*/
import java.awt.*; import
java.awt.event.*;
import java.applet.*;
public class RadioTest extends Applet
{
        public void init()
        {
                CheckboxGroup cbg = new CheckboxGroup();

                // Checkbox(label, specific checkgroup,checked:boolean) Checkbox c1
                = new Checkbox("Black and White",cbg,false);
                Checkbox c2 = new Checkbox("Color",cbg,false);
```

```
                    //adding mouselistener to the corresponding
                       // component to trap the event
                    c1.addMouseListener(new check1());
                    c2.addMouseListener(new check2());
                    //adding components to the container
                       add(c1);
                       add(c2);
              //To create a Choice Menu(say to list the various choices)
                      //a Choice Object is instantiated.

    //In short-Choice() constructor creates a new choice menu

    //& you add items using addITem()

              Choice c = new Choice(); c.add("LG");

              c.add("Onida"); c.add("BPL");

              c.add("Samsung"); c.add("Philips");

              c.add("Sony");

// adding ItemListener to choice then adding it to the container
              c.addItemListener(new Ch()); add(c);
              }

       Class check1 extends MouseAdapter
          {
              Public void mouseClicked(MouseEvent e)
              {
              showStatus("You have selected Black & White TV option");
               }
          }

       Class check2 extends MouseAdapter
          {
              Public void mouseClicked(MouseEvent e)
              {
                showStatus("You have selected Color TV option");
              }
          }

       Class Ch implements ItemListener
       {

    Public void itemStateChanged(ItemEvent e)
          {
              String s =(String)e.getItem();
               showStatus("You have selected" + s + " brand for
your TV");
              }
          }
}
```

13

SWING

Unit Structure
Introduction to JFC (Java Foundation Classes)
Swing
Swing Features
JComponent
JApplet
JFrame
JPannel
JButtons, checkboxes and Radiobuttons

13.1 INTRODUCTION TO JFC (JAVA FOUNDATION CLASSES)

The earlier versions of java were released with some simple libraries. JDK1.2 was introduced with a new set of packages – the java foundation classes, or JFC – that includes an improved user interface called the **swing** components.

The JFC were developed, to address the shortcomings of AWT(Abstract Windowing Toolkit). The development of JFC was unique. JFC 1.2 is an extension of the AWT, not a replacement for it. The JFC visual components extend the AWT container class. The methods contained in the component and container classes that AWT programmers are familiar with are still valid for JFC visual classes.

The AWT user interface classes are now superseded by classes provided by the JFC. The support classes play an important role in JFC applications . AWT support classes , those that do not create a native window are not replaced by JFC classes.

13.2 SWING

Swing components facilitate efficient graphical user interface (GUI) development. These components are a collection of lightweight visual components. Swing components contain a replacement for the heavyweight AWT components as well as complex user-interface components such as trees and tables.

Swing components contain a pluggable look and feel(PL&F). This allows all applications to run with the native look and feel on different platforms. PL&F allows applications to have the same behavior on various platforms. JFC contains operating systems neutral look and feel. Swing components do not contain peers. Swing components allow mixing AWT heavyweight and swing lightweight components in an application. The major difference between lightweight and heavyweight components is that lightweight components can have transparent pixels while heavyweight components are always opaque. Lightweight components can be non-regular while heavyweight components are always rectangular.
Swing components are JavaBean compliant. This allows components to be used easily in a Bean aware applications building program. The root of the majority of

Swing	AWT
Swing component does not need any native code to implement.	AWT component can implementing with code.
Swing lets you specify which look and feel your programs GUI uses.	AWT components always ha the look and feel of the nat platform.
Swing components don't have to be rectangular. For ex. Buttons can be rounded.	AWT components are alwa rectangular.

The swing architecture is shown in the figure given below.

Swing components comprises of a large percentage of the JFC release. The swing component toolkit consists of over 250 pure java classes and 75 interfaces contained in about 10 packages. They are used to build lightweight user interface. Swing consists of user interface(UI) classes and non user interface classes. The non-UI classes provide services and other operations for the UI classes.

Swing packages:
Some of the Swing packages are given below.

1. Javax.swing.plaf.basic : Contains classes that define the default look and feel of swing components.

2. Javax.swing.border : Contains border interface and their related interfaces.

3. Javax.swing. event: Define events specific to swing components.

4. Javax.swing.plaf.multi: Consist of multiplexing UI classes

5. Javax.swing.plaf: Consist of classes that provide swing components with pluggable look and feel capabilities.

6. Javax.swing.table: Contains classes and interfaces specific to the swing table components

7. Javax.swing.text: Contains classes and interfaces for text manipulation components contained in swing toolkit.

8. Javax.swing.tree: Contains classes that are used with the swing tree component

9. Javax.swing.undo: contains interfaces and classes required to implement the undo functionality.

13.3 SWING FEATURES :

MVC Architecture: The user can provide his own data-model for a component by subclassing the Model class or by implementing the appropriate interface. The Model-View-Controller (MVC) architecture is used consistently throughout the swing component set. The view and controller parts of the architecture are combined in the component.

Nested Containers: Swing was designed to manage nested containers gracefully. The main heavyweight containers(JWindow, JFrame etc.) as well as the major 'lightweight' containers(JInternalFrame and JComponent) all delegate their operations to a JRootPane. This commonly produces high degree of regularity in container nesting. In particular since the fundamental component class(JComponent) contains a JRootPane, virtually any component can be nested within another.

Keystroke Handling: A user can register interest in a particular combination of keystrokes by creating a keystroke object and registering it with the component. When the keystroke combination is registered along with its association action, certain conditions have to be specified. These determine the time of initiation of the action.

Action Objects: action interface objects provide a single point of control for program actions. An example of this would be a toolbar icon and a menu item referencing the same Action objects. When action object disabled, the GUI items that reference it are automatically disabled.

Virtual Desktops: The JdesktopPane and JInternalFrame classes can be used to create a virtual desktop or multiple document interface. A JInternalFrame can be specified as cognizable, expandable or closable, while the JDesktopPane Provides real estate for them to operate in.

Pluggable look and feel: The user can select a look and feel and this can be plugged in. An interface made of Swing components can look like a Win32 app, a Motif app. It can use the new Metal look and feel.

Wide variety of components: Class names that starts with J are the components that are added to and application. For ex. JButton, JList, JPanel.

13.4 J COMPONENT

The JComponent class is the root of the visual component class hierarchy in the JFC. The visual components are known as the "J" classes. The functionality contained in the Jcomponent class is available to all the visual components contained in the JFC. The JComponent class is repository of functionality for all visual components.

The JComponent class is at the top of the hierarchy of all visual components contained in the JFC. The hierarchy is shown in the following figure.

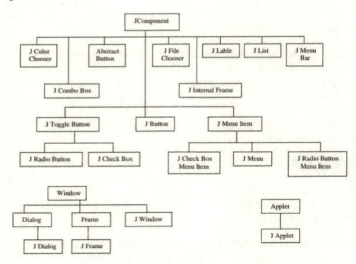

13.5 JAPPLET

The JApplet class is an extended version of the AWT applet class that adds support for root panes and other panes.. This class is the preferred entry point when creating applets that contain JFC components. The components are added to the ContentPane.

The constructor that can be used to create a JApplet are listed below:

JApplet() : It creates a swing applet instance

Some of the methods that can be used in conjunction with the JApplet is given below:

createRootPane( ): Called by the constructor methods to create the default root pane.

getContentPane( ) : Returns the content pane object for the applet

getGlassPane( ) : Returns the glass pane object for the applet getJMenuBar( ) : Returns the menu bar set on the applet

setContentPane( ) : sets the content pane properly

setGlassPane( ) : sets the glass pane properly

setLayout(LayoutManagermanager) : By default the layout of this component may not be set, the layout of its contentPane should be set instead.

13.6 J FRAME

Frame windows: A frame is a top-level window that contains a title, border, minimize and maximize buttons. JFC provides the JFrame class. This is used as a top-level-frame.

JFrame : A Swing frame is represented by the class Jframe, is an extension of the AWT Frame classes. It is the part of javax.swing package. A Swing frame is a container that functions as the main window for programs that use Swing components. An instance of the JFrame Class is a heavyweight component.

The JFrame can be created using the constructors mentioned below:

JFrame() : Constructs a new frame that is initially invisible.

JFrame(String title) : Constructs a new frame, initially invisible with the specified title.

Some of the methods that may be used in conjunction with the JFrame() are listed below:

createRootPane() : Called by the constructor methods to create the default root pane

frameInit() : Called by the constructor to init the JFrame properly.

getContentPane() : Returns the content pane object for this frame

getGlassPane() : Returns the glass pane object for this frame
getJMenuBar() : Returns the menu bar set on this frame
getLayeredPane() : Returns the layered pane for this frame

setContentPane() : Sets the content pane property

setGlassPane() : Sets the glass pane property

setJMenuBar() : Sets the menu bar for the frame

setLayout(LayoutManager manager) : By default the layout of this component may not be set, the layout of its contentPane should be set instead.

13.7 J PANNEL

JPanel is a Swing lightweight container that is often used for grouping components within one of an applet or a frame. It can also be used to group other panels. The primary purpose of the class is to provide a concrete container for the JFC. The JPanel class is provided to gibve a concrete container class. Being an extennsion of the Jcpmponent class, JPanel is a container and inherits the features contained in that class.

The various constructros that can be used to create a JPanel are as given below.

JPanel() : Create a new JPanel with a double buffer and a flow layout.

JPanel(Boolean is DoubleBuffered) : Create a new JPanel with FlowLayout and the specified buffering stratergy.

JPanel (LayoutManager layout) : create a buffered JPanel with the specified layout manager.

JPanel(LayoutManager layout, boolean is DoubleBuffered) : Creates a new JPanel with the specified layout manager and buffering stratergy.

The methods supported by this class includes :

getAccessibleContext() : Gets the AccessibleContext associated with this JComponent.

getUIClassID() : Returns a string that specifies the name of the L&F clss tht renders theis component.

paramString() : Returns a string representation of the corresponding JPanel.

update() : Notification fro the UIFactory that the L&F has changed.

13.8 JBUTTONS, CHECK BOXES AND RADIOBUTTONS

JButton: JButtons behaves In a way that is similar to Button. It can be added to JPanel and its actions can be monitored via the ActionListener. The JButton has to be pushed to make something happen. It consist of label and /or an icon that describes its function, an empty area around the text/icon and a border. By default, the border is a special border that reflects the status of the button.

A JButton can be constructed by any of the constructors mentioned below:

JButtons() : Creates a button with no text or icon

JButton(Icon icon) : Creates a button with icon.

JButton(String text) : Creates a button with text

JButton(String text, Icon icon) : Creates a button with text and icon

Some methods can be used in conjuctoin with a JButton are listed below:

isDefaultButton() : Returns whether or not the corresponding button is the default button on the RootPane.

isDefaultCapable() : Returns whether or not the corresponding button is capable of being the default button on the RootPane.

setDefaultCapable(booleandefaultCapable) : Sets whether or not the corresponding button is capable of being the default button on the RootPane.

Right-clicks on a Button

The default action of a JButton is to receive a left mouse click. The button could be programmed to receive a right mouse click also. There are ways in which this can be achived.

Creating our own UI for JButton

Overlay the button with an invisible component that would intercept all events and pass through all except right clicks.

Subclass JButton and override the process MouseEvent() method

JCheckBox: A JCheckBox is a control that may be turned on and off by the user to designate some kind of property being selected or not selected. It consist of a background rectangle, and a text string and/or icon. The JCheckBox normally shows its current state visually. This is done by placing a check mark in a box, or by changing the icon.

A JCheckbox generates item events when its state changes. The checkbox can be created by using any one of the constructors mentioned below:

JCheckBox() : Creates an initially unchecked checkbox with no text or icon.

JCheckBox(Icon icon) : Creates an initially unchecked checkbox with an icon.

JCheckBox(Icon icon, Boolean selected) : Creates a checkbox with an icon and specifies whether or not it is initially selected

JCheckBox(String text) : Creates an initially unchecked checkbox with the specified text.

JCheckBox(String text, Boolean selected) : Creates a checkbox with the specified text and specifies whether or not it is initially selected.

JCheckBox(String text, Icon icon) : Creates an initially unselected checkbox with the text and icon specified.

JCheckBox(String text, Icon icon, Boolean selected) : Creates a checkbox with icon and text and specifies whether or not it is initially selected.

JRadioButtons: This is normally used as one of a group of radio buttons of which only one may be selected at a time. These are grouped using a ButtonGroup and are usually used to select from a set of mutually exclusive options. It consists of a background rectangle and text and/or an icon. If it includes an icon, the icon is used to visually reflect the current state of the radio button.

Using the constructors listed below , radio buttons can be created:

JRadioButton() : Creates an initially unselected radio button with no set text.

JRadioButton(Icon icon) : Creates an initially unselected radio button with the specified image but no text.

JRadioButton(Icon icon, Boolean selected) : Creates a radio button with the specified image and selection state, but no text.

JRadioButton(String text) : Creates an initially unselected radio button with the specified text.

JRadioButton(String text, boolean selected) : Creates a radio button with specified text and selection state.

JRadioButton(String text, Icon icon) : Creates a radio button that has the specified text and image, and that is initially unselected.

JRadioButton(String text, Icon icon, boolean selected) : Creates a radio button that has the specified text, image, and selection state.

Programs:
Followig is the programm to display an Applet.

```java
import java.awt.event.*; import
java.awt.*; import javax.swing.*;
/*
<applet code = "Applets.class" width = 250 height = 250 > </applet>
*/
public class Applets extends JApplet
{
        JButton B1; public void init()
        {
                JPanel contentpane = (JPanel)getContentPane(); B1= new
                JButton("My First Applet"); contentpane.add(B1);
        }
}
```

Save the file as **Applets. Java**

Compile the file using **javac Applet.java**

On successful compilation, execute the file using
appletviewer Applets.java

The output appers as shown in following figure :

The following program is an example of Jframe/JButton

```java
import java.awt.*;
import java.awt.event.*;
import javax.swing.*;
public class Button1 extends JFrame implements ActionListener
{
        JButton mtextbtn1; JButton mtextbtn2;
        public Button1()
        {
                setTitle("Button Example");
                JPanel contentpane = (JPanel)getContentPane();
                contentpane.setLayout(new GridLayout(2,2));

                mtextbtn1= new JButton("Enabled");
                mtextbtn1.setMnemonic('E');
                mtextbtn1.addActionListener(this);
                contentpane.add(mtextbtn1);

                mtextbtn2 = new JButton("Disabled");
                mtextbtn2.setMnemonic('D');
                mtextbtn2.addActionListener(this);
                contentpane.add(mtextbtn2);
                mtextbtn1.setEnabled(true); myadapter myapp = new
                myadapter(); addWindowListener(myapp);
        }

        class myadapter extends WindowAdapter
        {
        public void windowclosing(WindowEvent e)
                {
                        System.exit(0);
                }
        }

public void actionPerformed(ActionEvent e)
{
        if (e.getSource() == mtextbtn1)
        {
                setTitle("First button clicked");
        }
        else if ( e.getSource() == mtextbtn2)
```

```
                {
                        setTitle("Second button clicked");
                }
        }

public static void main(String args[])
{
        Button1 b = new Button1(); b.setSize(100,100);
        b.setVisible(true);

}
}
```

Save the file as **Button1.java**
Compile the program using **javac Button1.java**
Execute the program using **java Button1**

The output appears as shown in following figure.

Example program for JCheckBoxes/JFrame.

```java
import java.awt.*;

import java.awt.event.*;

import javax.swing.*;

public class checkbox1 extends JFrame implements ItemListener
{
        JCheckBox checkbox; public
        checkbox1()
        {
                setTitle("Check box Example");
                JPanel contentpane = (JPanel)getContentPane();
                contentpane.setLayout(new GridLayout(2,2)); checkbox = new
                JCheckBox("Toggle"); checkbox.addItemListener(this);
                contentpane.add(checkbox);
                myadapter myapp = new myadapter();
                addWindowListener(myapp);
        }

class myadapter extends WindowAdapter
{
        public void windowclosing(WindowEvent e)
        {
                System.exit(0);
        }
}

public void itemStateChanged(ItemEvent e)
{
if (e.getStateChange() == ItemEvent.SELECTED)
{
        setTitle("Checkbox selected");
}
        else
{
        setTitle("Checkbox unselected");
}
}
public static void main(String args[])
{
        checkbox1 c = new checkbox1();
        c.setSize(250,250); c.setVisible(true);
}
}
```

Save the file as **checkbox1.java**

Compile the file using javac **checkbox1.java**

Execute the file using **java checkbox**

The output appears as shown in the follwing figure;

 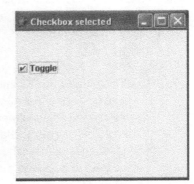

Example program for JRadioButtons

```
import java.awt.*;
import java.awt.event.*;
import javax.swing.*;
public class Radiobuttons extends JFrame implements ItemListener

{

        JRadioButton rb1, rb2;

        ButtonGroup grp = new ButtonGroup();
        public Radiobuttons()

        {

        setTitle("Radio Buttons Example");
        JPanel contentpane = (JPanel)getContentPane();
        contentpane.setLayout(new FlowLayout());

        rb1 = new JRadioButton("Enabled");
        rb1.addItemListener(this); rb1.setEnabled(true);
        contentpane.add(rb1);
        rb2 = new JRadioButton("Disabled");

        rb2.addItemListener(this); //rb2.setActionCommand("Two Activated");

        contentpane.add(rb2);

        rb2.setEnabled(false);

        grp.add(rb1);
```

194

```
                grp.add(rb2);

                myadapter myapp = new myadapter();
                addWindowListener(myapp);
                }
class myadapter extends WindowAdapter
{
                public void windowClosing(WindowEvent e)
                {
                        System.exit(0);
                }
}
public void itemStateChanged(ItemEvent e)
{
                if (e.getSource()==rb1)
                {
                        setTitle("First radio button enabled");
                        rb1.setEnabled(false); rb2.setEnabled(true);
                }
                        else if(e.getSource()==rb2)

                {
                        setTitle("Second radio button enabled");
                        rb1.setEnabled(true);
                        rb2.setEnabled(false);
                }
}
public static void main(String args[])
                {
                Radiobuttons rb = new Radiobuttons();
                rb.setSize(300,300); rb.setVisible(true);

                }
}
```

Save the file as **Radiobuttons.java**
Compile the file using **javac Radiobuttons.java**
On successful compilation execute the file using
Java Radiobuttons
The output appears as shown in the following figure :

14

JDBC ARCHITECTURE

Unit Structure
Introduction to JDBC
Java and JDBC
JDBC VS ODBC
JDBC DRIVER MODEL
JDBC Driver Types
Two-tier Architecture for Data Access
Three-tier Architecture for Data Access
SQL CONFORMANCE
Types of Driver Managers

14.1 INTRODUCTION TO JDBC

JDBC stands for Java Database Connectivity. It is set of Java API's(application programming interface) used for executing SQL statements. This API consists of a set of classes and interfaces to enable programmers to write pure Java Database applications.

JDBC is a software layer that allows developers to write real client –server projects in Java. JDBC does not concern itself with specific DBMS functions. JDBC API defines how an application opens a connection, communicates with a database, executes SQL statements, and retrieves query result. Following fig. will illustrate the role of JDBC. JDBC is based on the X/OPEN call level interface (CLI) for SQL.

Call Level Interface is a library of function calls that supports SQL statements. CLI requires neither host variables nor other embedded SQL concepts that would make it less flexible from a programmer's perspective. It is still possible, however, to maintain and use specific functions of a database management system when accessing the database through a CLI.

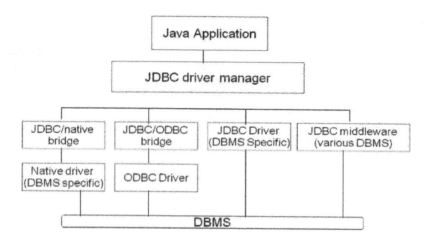

JDBC was designed to be very compact, simple interface focusing on the execution of raw SQL statements and retrieving the results. The goal of creating JDBC is to create an interface that keeps simple tasks, while ensuring the more difficult and uncommon tasks are at least made possible.

The following are the characteristics of JDBC.

1. It is a call-level SQL interface for java
2. It does not restrict the type of queries passed to an underlying DBMS driver
3. JDBC mechanism are simple to understand and use
4. It provides a java interface that stays consistent with the rest of the Java system
5. JDBC may be implemented on top of common SQL level APIs.

Microsoft ODBC API offers connectivity to almost all databases on all platforms and is the most widely used programming interface for accessing relational database. But ODBC cannot be directly used with java programs due to various reasons enumerated in the JDBC vs. ODBC section. Hence the need for JDBC came into existence.

It is possible to access various relational databases like Sybase, Oracle, Informix, Ingers, using JDBC API. Using JDBC, we can write individual programs to connect to individual database or one program that take care of connecting to the respective database.

14.2 JAVA AND JDBC

The combination of java with JDBC is very useful because it lets the programmer run his/her program on different platforms, Java programs are secure, robust, automatically downloaded from the network and java is a good language to create database applications. JDBC API enables Java applications to interact with different types of database. It is possible to publish vital information from a remote database on a web page using a java applet. With increasing inclination of programmers towards Java, knowledge about JDBC is essential.

Some of the advantages of using Java with JDBC are as follows:

> Easy and economical
> Continued usage of already installed databases
> Development time is short
> Installation and version control simplified

How does JDBC work

JDBC defines a set of API objects and methods to interact with the underlying database. A Java program first opens a connection to the database, makes a statement object, passes SQL statements to the underlying database management system (DBMS) through the statement object and retrieve the results as well as information about the result set.

There are two types of interfaces – low –level interface and high-level interface. While high level interfaces are user-friendly, low-level interfaces are not. JDBC is a low-level API interface, ie. it used to invoke or call SQL commands directly. The required SQL statements are passed as strings to Java methods.

Some of the current trend that are being developed to add more features to JDBC are embedded SQL for java and direct mapping of relational database to java classes.

Embedded SQL enables mixing of java into SQL statements. These statements are translated into JDBC calls using SQL Processor. In this type of direct mapping of relational database tables to java, each row of the table becomes an instance of the class and each column value corresponds to an attribute of that instance. Mapping is being provided that makes rows of multiple tables to form a java class.

14.3 JDBC VS ODBC

The most widely used interface to access relational database today is Microsoft's ODBC API. ODBC performs similar tasks as that of JDC(Java Development Connection) and yet JDBC is preferred due to the following reasons :

ODBC cannot be directly used with Java because it uses a C interface. Calls from Java to native C code have a number of drawbacks in the security, implementation, robustness and automatic portability of applications.

ODBC makes use of pointers which have been totally removed from Java

ODBC mixes simple and advanced features together and has complex options for simple queries. But JDBC is designed to keep things simple while allowing advanced capabilities when required.

JDBC API is a natural Java Interface and is built on ODBC. JDBC retains some of the basic features of ODBC like X/Open SQL Call Level Interface.

JDBC is to Java programs and ODBC is to programs written in languages other than Java.

ODBC is used between applications and JDBC is used by Java programmers to connect to databases.

Details about JDBC

The JDBC API is in the package java.sql it consists of 8 interfaces, 6 classes and 3 exceptions in JDK1.1.

Interfaces:
- CallableStatement
- Connection
- DatabaseMetaData
- Driver
- PreparedStatement
- ResultSet
- ResultSetMetaData
- Statement

Classes:
- Date
- DriverManager
- DriverPropertyInfo
- Time
- Timestamp
- Types

Exceptions:
- DataTruncation
- SQLException
- SQLWarning

14.4 JDBC DRIVER MODEL

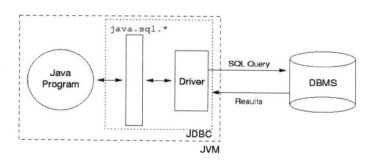

14.5 JDBC DRIVER TYPES

There are 4 types of JDBC drivers. Commonest and most efficient of which are type 4 drivers. Here is the description of each of them:

JDBC Type 1 Driver - They are JDBC-ODBC Bridge drivers ie. Translate JDBC into ODBC and use Windows ODBC built in drivers. They delegate the work of data access to ODBC API. They are the slowest of all. SUN provides a JDBC/ODBC driver implementation.

JDBC Type 2 Driver - They mainly use native API for data access ie. Converts JDBC to data base vendors native SQL calls and provide Java wrapper classes to be able to be invoked using JDBC drivers like Type 1 drivers; requires installation of binaries on each client.

JDBC Type 3 Driver - Translates JDBC to a DBMS independent network protocol. They are written in 100% Java and use vendor independent Net-protocol to access a vendor independent remote listener. This listener in turn maps the vendor independent calls to vender dependent ones. This extra step adds complexity and decreases the data access efficiency.

JDBC Type 4 Driver - They are also written in 100% Java and are the most efficient among all driver types. It compiles into the application, applet or servlet; doesn't require anything to be installed on client machine, except JVM. It also converts JDBC directly to native API used by the RDBMS.

The JDBC API supports both two-tier and three-tier processing models for database access.

14.6 TWO-TIER ARCHITECTURE FOR DATA ACCESS

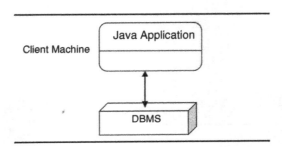

In the two-tier model, a Java application talks directly to the data source. This requires a JDBC driver that can communicate with the particular data source being accessed. A user's commands are delivered to the database or other data source, and the results of those statements are sent back to the user. The data source may be located on another machine to which the user is connected via a network. This is referred to as a client/server configuration, with the user's machine as the client, and the machine housing the data source as the server. The network can be an intranet, which, for example, connects employees within a corporation, or it can be the Internet.

In the three-tier model, commands are sent to a "middle tier" of services, which then sends the commands to the data source. The data source processes the commands and sends the results back to the middle tier, which then sends them to the user. MIS directors find the three-tier model very attractive because the middle tier makes it possible to maintain control over access and the kinds of updates that can be made to corporate data. Another advantage is that it simplifies the deployment of applications. Finally, in many cases, the three-tier architecture can provide performance advantages.

14.7 THREE-TIER ARCHITECTURE FOR DATA ACCESS

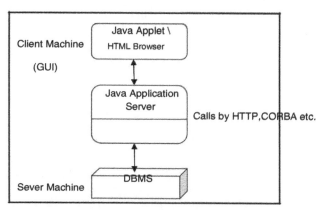

Until recently, the middle tier has often been written in languages such as C or C++, which offer fast performance. However, with the introduction of optimizing compilers that translate Java byte code into efficient machine-specific code and technologies such as Enterprise JavaBeans™, the Java platform is fast becoming the standard platform for middle-tier development. This is a big plus, making it possible to take advantage of Java's robustness, multithreading, and security features.

With enterprises increasingly using the Java programming language for writing server code, the JDBC API is being used more and more in the middle tier of a three-tier architecture. Some of the features that make JDBC a server technology are its support for connection pooling, distributed transactions, and disconnected row sets. The JDBC API is also what allows access to a data source from a Java middle tier.

14.8 SQL CONFORMANCE

Structured Query Language (SQL) is the standard language used to access relational databases, unfortunately, there are no standards set at present for it for ex, problems may arise due to the variations in different data types of different databases. JDBC defines a set of generic SWL types identifiers in the class Java.SQL.Types

Ways of dealing with SQL conformance

JDBC deals with SQL conformance by performing the following :

JDBC API allows any query string to be passed through to an underlying DBMS driver. But there are possibilities of getting an error on some DBMS.

Provision of ODBC style escape closes.

Provision of descriptive information about the DBMS using an interface, DatabaseMetaData.

The designation JDBC Compliant was created to set a standard level of JDBC functionality on which users can rely. Only the ANSI SQL 2 enty level supported drivers can make use of this designation. The conformance tests check for the existence of all classes and methods defined in the JDBC API and SQL entry level functionality.

14.9 TYPES OF DRIVER MANAGERS

JDBC contains three components: Application, Driver Manager, Driver. The user application invokes JDBC methods to send SQL statements to the database and retrieves results. JDBC driver manager is used to connect Java applications to the correct JDBC driver . JDBC driver test suite is used to ensure that the installed JDBC driver is JDBC Compliant. There are four different types of JDBC drivers as follows

1. The JDBC-ODBC Bridge plus ODBC driver :

The JDBC-ODBC Bridge plus ODBC driver is a JavaSoft Bridge protocol that provides JDBC access via ODBC drivers. But as we have mentioned earlier, combining ODBC brings in a lot of drawbacks and limitations, since the ODBC driver has to be installed on each client machine, it is not advisable to choose this type of driver for large networks.

2. Native-API partly-Java driver :

Native-API partly-Java driver converts JDBC calls into calls on the client API for Oracle, Sybase, Informix or other DBMS. But some binary code has to be loaded on all client like the bridge driver and hence is not suitable for large networks.

3.JDBC-Net pure Java driver:

JDBC-Net pure Java driver translates JDBC calls into DBMS independent net protocol. A server again translates this protocol to a DBMS protocol. The net server middleware connects its pure Java clients to many different databases. The type of protocol in this middleware depends on the vendor.

4. Native-protocol pure Java driver :
Native-protocol pure Java driver convert JDBC calls to network protocols used by the DBMSs directly. Requests from client machines are made directly to the DBMS server.

Drivers 3 and 4 are the most preferred ways to access databases from JDBC drivers.

DATABASE CONNECTIVITY

Unit Structure
Introduction
A connection can be open with the help of following steps
Connecting to an ODBC Data Source
JDBC Programs

15.1 INTRODUCTION :

A Database connection is a facility in computer science that allows client software to communicate with database server software, whether on the same machine or not. A connection is required to send commands and receive answers.

Connections are built by supplying an underlying driver or provider with a connection string, which is a way of addressing a specific database or server and instance as well as user authentication credentials (for example, *Server=sql_box;Database =Common;User ID=uid;Pwd=password;*). Once a connection has been built it can be opened and closed at will, and properties (such as the command time-out length, or transaction, if one exists) can be set. The Connection String is composed of a set of key/value pairs as dictated by the data access interface and data provider being used.

15.2 A CONNECTION CAN BE OPEN WITH THE HELP OF FOLLOWING STEPS

1. Importing Packages

2. Registering the JDBC Drivers

3. Opening a Connection to a Database

4. Creating a Statement Object

5. Executing a Query and Returning a Result Set Object

6. Processing the Result Set

7. Closing the Result Set and Statement Objects

8. Closing the Connection

Step 1. Importing Packages
The following JDBC packages will be imported for creating connection.
java.sql.
java.math.
java.io.
oracle.jdbc.driver.

Step 2. Registering the JDBC Drivers

Following four parameters are required to register JDBC Drivers. o Database URL

o JDBC Driver name
o User Name
o   Password

JDBC Drivers can be register using following methods. o Class drvClass=Class.forName(m_driverName);
DriverManager.registerDriver((Driver)drvClass.newInstance ());

Step 3 : Opening a Connection to a Database

Connection to the underlying database can be opened using

Connection m_con=DriverManager.getConnection(m_url,m_userName,m_pass word) ;

Step 4 : Creating a Statement Object

SQL Statements

Once a connection is established, It is used to pass SQL statements to its underlying database. JDBC provides three classes for sending SQL Statements to the database, where PreparedStatement extends from Statement, and CallableStatement extends from PreparedStatement:

Statement	: For simple SQL statements (no parameter)
PreparedStatement	: For SQL statements with one or more IN parameters, or simple SQL statements that are executed frequently.
CallableStatement	: For executing SQL stored procedures.

The statement interface provides three different methods for **executing SQL statements** :

executeQuery	: For statements that produce a single result set.
executeUpdate	: For executing **INSERT, UPDATE**, or **DELETE** statements and also **SQL DDL** (Data Definition Language) statements.
execute	: For executing statements that return more than one result set, more than one update count, or a combination of the two.

A Statement object is used with following steps:

Statement
Statement stmt=m_con.createStatement();
Statement stmt=m_con.createStatement(int resultSetType, int resultSetConcurrency);

PreparedStatement
PreparedStatement pstmt=m_con.prepareStatement(String sql); PreparedStatement pstmt=m_con.prepareStatement(String sql, int resultSetType,int resultSetConcurrency),

Note:
The SQL parameter could contain one or more '?' in it. Before a PreparedStatement object is executed, the value of each '?' parameter must be set by calling a setXXX method, where XXX stands for appropriate type for the parameter. For ex. If the parameter has a java type of String, the method to use is setString.

CallableStatement
CallableStatemet csmt=m_con.prepareCall(String sql); CallableStatemet csmt=m_con.prepareCall(String sql, int resultSetType, int resultSetConcurrency),);

Note :
The sql parameter is in the form of "{call <stored_procedure_name>[(arg1, arg2,...)]} " or" { ?=call <stored_procedure_name>[(arg1,arg2...)]}". It could contain one or more '?'s in it, which indiacates IN, OUT or INOUT parameters. The value of each IN parameter is set by calling a setXXX mehod, while each OUT parameter should be registered by calling a registerOutParameter method.

Step 5: Executing a Query and Returning a Result Set Object AND
Step 6: Processing the Result set

Execute the Statement

Statement :
ResultSet res=stmt.executeQuery(String sql);
int rowCount=stmt.executeUpdate(String sql);
boolean result=stmt.execute(String sql);

PrepaedStatement :
ResultSet res=pstmt.executeQuery();
int rowCount=pstmt.executeUpdate();
boolean result=pstmt.execute();

CallableStatement :
ResultSet res=cstmt.executeQuery();
int rowCount=cstmt.executeUpdate();
boolean result=cstmt.execute();

Processing the Result set

A result set contains all of the rows which satisfied the conditions in an SQL statement and it provides access to the data in those rows through getXXX mehods that allow access to the various columns of the current row.

The ResultSet.next() method is used to move to the next row of the ResultSet, making the next row become the current row. ResultSet.next() returns true if the new current row is valid, false if there are no more rows. After all the works have been done, the ResultSet should be closed with ResultSet.close() method.

Because of limitations imposed by some DBMSs, it is recommended that for maximum portability, all of the results generated by the execution of a CallableStatement object should be retrieved before OUT parameters are retrieved using CallableStatement.getXXX methods.

Step 7: Closing the Result Set and Statement Objects

Close the statement
After all the works have been done, the result set and statement should be closed with the following code

```
Resultset          : rset.close();
Statement          : stmt.close();
PrepaedStatement : pstmt.close();
CallableStatement : cstmt.close();
```

Step 8: Closing the Connection
After all the works have been done, the Connection should be closed with the following code:
Connection name)m_con.close();

15.3 CONNECTING TO AN ODBC DATA SOURCE
A database can be created and managed through Java applications. Java application that uses a JDBC-ODBC bridge to connect to a database file either a dbase, Excel, FoxPro, Access, SQL Server, Oracle or any other. Open the ODBC Data source from the control panel. A database can be created and managed through Java applications.
Follow the following steps to connect to an ODBC Data Source for "ORACLE".
Select Control Panel.

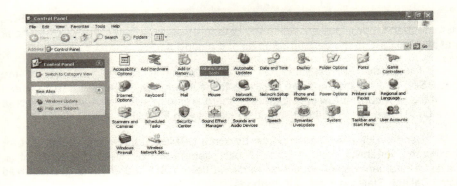

Select "Data Sources (ODBC)" icon

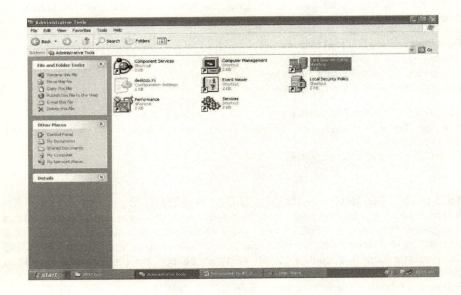

208

4. Select the MS-ODBC for oracle or any other driver that felt it required.

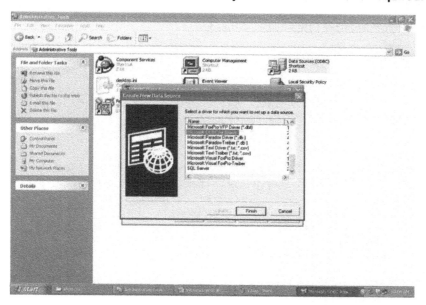

5. Once clicking the finish button, the following window appears asking for Data Source name, description etc.

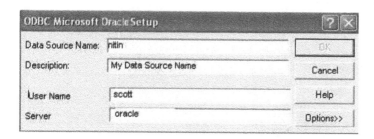

Provide "Data Source Name", "Discription","Username" and "Server" name. The username and Server name can be obtained from the Administrator. Click on ok button.

The DSN is now ready and the Java code can be written to access the database's tables.

15.4 JDBC PROGRAMS

1. Example for creating Table.

```
// Create Table
import java.sql.*;          // imports all classes that belongs to the
package java.sql.*
public class CreateTab
{
        public static void main(String args[ ])
        {
                try
                {
        Class.forName("sun.jdbc.odbc.JdbcOdbcDriver"); Connectioncon=
                DriverManager.getConnection
                                (jdbc:odbc:nitin" ,scott","tiger"); // specifies the
                type of driver as JdbcOdbcDriver.
        Statement stat= con.createStatement(); String str="Create table T1(Rno
        number(2), Stdname varchar2(20))"; Stat.executeUpdate(str);
        System.out.println("Table created successfully");
        }
        Catch(SQLExecution e 1)
        {
                System.out.println("Errors" + e 1);
        }
        Catch(ClassNotFoundException e 2)
        {
                System.out.println("Errors" + e 2);
        }
  }
}
```

2.Example for inserting records into a Table

```
// Insert into table
import java.sql.*;
public class InsertTab
{
        public static void main(String args[])
        {
        ResultSet result;
                try
                {

        Class.forName("sun.jdbc.odbc.JdbcOdbcDriver");
                                Connectioncon= DriverManager.getConnection
                        (jdbc:odbc:nitin" ,scott","tiger");

        Statement stat= con.createStatement();

        Stat.executeUpdate("Insert into T1 values(20,'Smith')");
        Stat.executeUpdate("Insert into T1 values(21,'John')");
```

```
Stat.executeUpdate("Insert into T1 values(22,'Kate')");
Stat.executeUpdate("Insert into T1 values(23,'Stive')");

System.out.println(Rows Inserted successfully");

result=stat.executeQuery("Select * from T1");

while(result.next())
{

System.out.println(result.getInt(l)+result.getString(2));
}
}
catch(Exception e)
{
System.out.println("Errors"+e);
}
}
}
```

3.Example for viewing rows from a table

```
// viwing from emp table
import java.sql.*;
public class SelectEmp
{
    public stativ void main(String args[])
    {
        String url="jdbc:odbc:nitin"; Connection con;
        String s= "select ename from emp 1"; Statement stmt;
    try
    {
        Class.forName("sun.jdbc.odbc.JdbcOdbcDriver");
    }
    catch(java.lang.ClassNotFoundException e)
    {
        System.err.println("ClassNotFoundException:");
        System.err.println(e.getMessage());
    }

    try
    {

con=DriverManager.getConnection(url,"Scott","Tiger");

        stmt=con.createStatement();

        resultSet rs=stmt.executeQuery(s);

        while(rs.next())
        {
            String s1=rs.getString("ename");

            System.out.println("Employee name:" +s1);
```

```
            }
            stmt.close();
            con.close();
        }
    catch(SQLException ex)
    {
    System.err.println("SQLException:"+ex.getMessage());
    }
    }
}
```

4. Example using prepared statements

```
import java.sql.*;
public class PreStExample
{
        public static void main(String[] args)
        {
        Connection con = null; PreparedStatement
        prest; try{
        Class.forName("sun.jdbc.odbc.JdbcOdbcDriver");
        Connectioncon= DriverManager.getConnection(jdbc:odbc:nitin"
,scott","tiger");
        try{
String sql = "SELECT stdname FROM T1 WHERE Rno = ?"; prest =
        con.prepareStatement(sql);
        prest.setInt(1,21);
        ResultSet rs1 = prest.executeQuery(); while (rs1.next())
        {
        String stname = rs1.getString(1);

            System.out.println("student name is: "+stname);
        }
        prest.setInt(1,23);
        ResultSet rs2 = prest.executeQuery(); while (rs2.next())
        {
        String stname1 = rs2.getString(1);

            System.out.println("student name is: "+stname1);
        }
        }
        catch (SQLException s){
                                System.out.println("SQL statement is not executed!");
        }
        }
        catch (Exception e){
        e.printStackTrace();
        }
        }
}
```

Lambda expressions are introduced in Java 8 and are biggest feature of Java 8 that facilitate functional programming, and simplifies the development a lot.The Lambda expression is used to provide the implementation of an interface which has functional interface. It saves a lot of code. In case of lambda expression, we don't need to define the method again for providing the implementation. Here, we just write the implementation code.Java lambda expression is treated as a function, so compiler does not create .class file.

Functional Interface

Lambda expression provides implementation of *functional interface*. An interface which has only one abstract method is called functional interface. Java provides an anotation *@FunctionalInterface*, which is used to declare an interface as functional interface.

Why use Lambda Expression

1. To provide the implementation of Functional interface.
2. Less coding.

Syntax

A lambda expression is characterized by the following syntax.

parameter -> expression body

Java lambda expression is consisted of three components.

1) Argument-list: It can be empty or non-empty as well.

2) Arrow-token: It is used to link arguments-list and body of expression.

3) Body: It contains expressions and statements for lambda expression.

Following are the important characteristics of a lambda expression.

Optional type declaration – No need to declare the type of a parameter. The compiler can inference the same from the value of the parameter.

Optional parenthesis around parameter – No need to declare a single parameter in parenthesis. For multiple parameters, parentheses are required.

Optional curly braces – No need to use curly braces in expression body if the body contains a single statement.

Optional return keyword – The compiler automatically returns the value if the body has a single expression to return the value. Curly braces are required to indicate that expression returns a value.

Lambda Expressions Example

Java8Tester.java

```
public class Tester
{
  public static void main(String args[])
  {
    Tester tester = new Tester();
    //with type declaration
    MathOperation addition = (int a, int b) -> a + b;
    //with out type declaration
    MathOperation subtraction = (a, b) -> a - b;
    //with return statement along with curly braces
    MathOperation multiplication = (int a, int b) -> { return a * b; };
    //without return statement and without curly braces
    MathOperation division = (int a, int b) -> a / b;
    System.out.println("10 + 5 = " + tester.operate(10, 5, addition));
    System.out.println("10 - 5 = " + tester.operate(10, 5, subtraction));
    System.out.println("10 x 5 = " + tester.operate(10, 5, multiplication));
    System.out.println("10 / 5 = " + tester.operate(10, 5, division));
    //without parenthesis
    GreetingService greetService1 = message ->
    System.out.println("Hello " + message);
    //with parenthesis
    GreetingService greetService2 = (message) ->
    System.out.println("Hello " + message);
    greetService1.sayMessage("Ajit");
    greetService2.sayMessage("Singh");
  }

  interface MathOperation
  {
    int operation(int a, int b);
  }

  interface GreetingService
  {
    void sayMessage(String message);
  }
```

```
    private int operate(int a, int b, MathOperation mo)
    {
      return mo.operation(a, b);
    }
}
```

Verify the Result

Compile the class using **javac** compiler as follows –

C:\JAVA>javac Tester.java
Now run the Tester as follows –

C:\JAVA>java Tester
It should produce the following output –

10 + 5 = 15
10 - 5 = 5
10 x 5 = 50
10 / 5 = 2
Hello Ajit
Hello Signh

Following are the important points to be considered in the above example.

Lambda expressions are used primarily to define inline implementation of a functional interface, i.e., an interface with a single method only. In the above example, we've used various types of lambda expressions to define the operation method of MathOperation interface. Then we have defined the implementation of sayMessage of GreetingService.

Lambda expression eliminates the need of anonymous class and gives a very simple yet powerful functional programming capability to Java.

Scope

Using lambda expression, you can refer to any final variable or effectively final variable (which is assigned only once). Lambda expression throws a compilation error, if a variable is assigned a value the second time.

Scope Example

Tester.java

```
public class Java8Tester
{
```

```java
final static String salutation = "Hello! ";
public static void main(String args[])
{

   GreetingService greetService1 = message ->
   System.out.println(salutation + message);
   greetService1.sayMessage("Ajit");

}
interface GreetingService
{

   void sayMessage(String message);

}
}
```

Verify the Result

Compile the class using **javac** compiler as follows –

C:\JAVA>javac Tester.java
Now run the Java8Tester as follows –

C:\JAVA>java Tester
It should produce the following output –

Hello! Ajit

Java 8 introduces a new concept of default method implementation in interfaces. This capability is added for backward compatibility so that old interfaces can be used to leverage the lambda expression capability of Java 8.

For example, 'List' or 'Collection' interfaces do not have 'forEach' method declaration. Thus, adding such method will simply break the collection framework implementations. Java 8 introduces default method so that List/Collection interface can have a default implementation of forEach method, and the class implementing these interfaces need not implement the same.

Syntax

```java
public interface vehicle {
  default void print() {
    System.out.println("I am a vehicle!");
  }
}
```

Multiple Defaults

With default functions in interfaces, there is a possibility that a class is implementing two interfaces with same default methods. The following code explains how this ambiguity can be resolved.

```java
public interface vehicle {

  default void print() {
    System.out.println("I am a vehicle!");
  }
}


public interface fourWheeler {

  default void print() {
    System.out.println("I am a four wheeler!");
  }
}
```

First solution is to create an own method that overrides the default implementation.

```java
public class car implements vehicle, fourWheeler {
```

```
  public void print() {
    System.out.println("I am a four wheeler car vehicle!");
  }
}
```

Second solution is to call the default method of the specified interface using super.

```
public class car implements vehicle, fourWheeler {

  default void print() {
    vehicle.super.print();
  }
}
```

Static Default Methods

An interface can also have static helper methods from Java 8 onwards.

```
public interface vehicle {

  default void print() {
    System.out.println("I am a vehicle!");
  }

  static void blowHorn() {
    System.out.println("Blowing horn!!!");
  }
}
```

Default Method Example

```
public class Tester {
  public static void main(String args[]) {
    Vehicle vehicle = new Car();
    vehicle.print();
  }
}

interface Vehicle {
  default void print() {
    System.out.println("I am a vehicle!");
  }

  static void blowHorn() {
    System.out.println("Blowing horn!!!");
  }
```

```
  }

interface FourWheeler {
  default void print() {
    System.out.println("I am a four wheeler!");
  }
}

class Car implements Vehicle, FourWheeler {
  public void print() {
    Vehicle.super.print();
    FourWheeler.super.print();
    Vehicle.blowHorn();
    System.out.println("I am a car!");
  }
}
```

Verify the Result

Compile the class using **javac** compiler as follows –

C:\JAVA>javac Tester.java

Now run the Java8Tester as follows –

C:\JAVA>java Tester

It should produce the following output –

I am a vehicle!
I am a four wheeler!
Blowing horn!!!
I am a car!

Thank You !!

220

www.ingramcontent.com/pod-product-compliance
Lightning Source LLC
LaVergne TN
LVHW042333060326

832902LV00006B/151